Max Bonnell is a Sydney lawyer and author, who writes on law, history, the performing arts and sport. He has, on three occasions, won the Jack Pollard Trophy, awarded annually to the best book on Australian cricket.

Wilton St Hill and Learie Constantine were more than makers of runs and takers of wickets to the people of Trinidad and Tobago. Who will write a biography of Sir Donald Bradman must be able to write a history of Australia in the same period.

CLR James, *Beyond a Boundary*

A LONG WAY TO GO

The West Indies cricket team in Australia, 1930-31

MAX BONNELL

ETT IMPRINT
Exile Bay

First published by ETT Imprint, Exile Bay 2024

ETT IMPRINT
PO Box R1906
Royal Exchange NSW 1225 Australia

ISBN 978-1-923024-94-6 (lim ed)
ISBN 978-1-923024-95-3 (paper)
ISBN 978-1-923024-96-0 (ebook)

Cover: The West Indies Cricket Team in Adelaide

Design by Tom Thompson

CONTENTS

The team, as photographed by Crown Studios, Wellington.
New Zealand National Library.

1

An Invitation

In September 1928, the members of the Australian Board of Control for Cricket gathered in Sydney for their annual meeting. They engaged in some minor tinkering with the schedule for the imminent Marylebone Cricket Club tour, moving the match with Victoria forward by a day to avoid a clash with the Melbourne Cup. They decided that Australia's Test team would be chosen by a panel of four selectors, none of whom would be permitted to write for the press. They set the umpires' fees for international matches. And they resolved to invite a team from the West Indies to tour Australia in the 1929-30 season.

Politely, and with regret, the West Indies Board of Control declined the invitation: it had already made arrangements with MCC for a visit by an English team in 1929-30. Acting with its customary speed and agility, the Australian Board then suggested, at its annual meeting twelve months later, that a tour in 1930-31 might be possible. That invitation was accepted promptly, although not before the West Indies Board of Control reached agreement with the MCC to defer its planned 1932 tour to England by a year.

More than fifty years had passed since the first Test match had been played, and in that time Australia had played Tests only against England and South Africa. The arrival of a new opponent was exciting, and the West Indian team was regarded as an exotic novelty. Very few people in Australia, however, had any real idea of what the West Indies were.

The concept of a West Indies cricket team had existed since at least 1900, when a team of players from Trinidad, Barbados and British Guiana visited England. A second tour, in 1906, included a couple of Jamaicans. But it was far from clear who or what the West Indies represented – it wasn't a country, or even a clearly-defined region, and the team was assembled on an ad hoc basis rather than by any permanent governing body. The power in the game lay with the prominent clubs in each colony – such as the Queen's Park Club in Trinidad and the Melbourne

Englishman Harry Mallett, manager of the West Indies team.

Joe Scheult, a Trinidad bank manager and father of ten, acted as assistant manager.

Club in Kingston – which, by reason of their substantial membership fees, tended to be socially exclusive.

West Indies cricket began as a colonial construction, fashioned to a paternalistic English design. There had never been any pressing local demand for the creation of a West Indies cricket team: instead, it was formed in the same way that new African countries were – by men sitting in offices in London, joining things together on maps. It was a Marylebone Cricket Club member, Harry Mallett, who convened the first meeting of the West Indies Cricket Conference, in Bridgetown in January 1927. Mallett had been an enthusiastic cricketer for Durham, and a driving force behind the formation of the Minor Counties Cricket Association. In winter, he played Rugby Union and soccer, and he achieved a small measure of fame by playing for Darlington at both sports on the same afternoon in 1889. He played a single first-class cricket match, for MCC against London County, which was memorable mostly because he was dismissed, in his only innings, by WG Grace. During his five years on the MCC committee, he was a vigorous advocate for the development of the game in the West Indies, and he had been appointed as manager of the West Indian tours to England in 1906 and 1923, a role he filled again in 1928..

Mallett's conference resolved to form a West Indies Cricket Board of Control, which was to consist of two representatives from each of Barbados, Jamaica, Trinidad and British Guiana, one from the Windward Islands, and one from the Leeward Islands. The Board of Control, which met for the first time in June 1929, was granted membership of the Imperial Cricket Conference, meaning that any matches it played against England, Australia and South Africa would be regarded as Tests. The West Indies played their first three Tests during their 1928 tour of England, losing each game by an innings and more.

The Imperial Cricket Conference did not acquire its name by accident. A condition of membership was allegiance to the British Crown. Even if, say, France had developed extraordinary cricketing strength, it could never have been admitted to play Test cricket, because it

George Headley.

would not satisfy the primary qualification. When South Africa declared itself a republic in 1961, it was banished from the ICC, which decreed that future matches between South Africa and its members would be 'unofficial' Tests only. Just as the British Empire was administered from Whitehall, the ICC met, always and only, at Lord's.

Harry Mallett's fingerprints are all over the imperial administration of cricket in this period: it was Mallett who drew up the Australian team's itinerary in England in 1930, and Mallett who represented Australia at meetings of the ICC, although he had never set foot in Australia, The concept of a West Indies team made perfect sense to Mallett, who saw all of the British colonies in the Caribbean as essentially similar, cricket-playing, components of the Empire. The idea was less immediately appealing to the players themselves. If a cricketer from Barbados spoke of the national team, he meant the Barbados team. There was no obvious reason why a black descendant of slaves in Jamaica should feel any sense of common identity with a white descendant of Portuguese planters, a thousand miles away in Demerara. It was easy enough to fit out a cricket team in burgundy caps and blazers, but creating a genuine shared purpose was a greater challenge than Mallett imagined.

It didn't help that the West Indian colonies didn't even play against each other all that often. There was an intercolonial tournament, but it wasn't staged every season and, when one was played, it excluded Jamaica. Between 1896 and 1929, Jamaica and Barbados didn't play each other even once. Jamaica and Trinidad didn't meet at all between 1908 and 1939. All of this created two serious handicaps for the West Indies. When a team was selected, as the Jamaican batsman George Headley put it, 'it must to some extent be thrown together' as a 'scratch team'. Many of the players were strangers to each other. And that 'scratch team' could be hindered by internal divisions, because players and administrators owed their primary loyalty to their homeland, rather than to the vague imperial concept of the West Indies.

The two boards negotiated the terms of the tour. There would be five Tests, two matches against each State (except, due to geographical constraints, Queensland, who received only one and Western Australia, who received none at all), and a couple of matches in the country. The West Indies

Board was responsible for paying the costs of its team, and would receive fifty percent of the gate receipts from each game. The Australian Board of Control agreed to pay a guarantee of up to £3000 in the event of a shortfall. 'But', the *Kingston Gleaner* cheerfully reported, 'it is not anticipated that there will be one, because, although £11,000 is the probable cost of the tour, the attractiveness of the West Indians ought to be worth at least £11,000.'[1]

That didn't, at the time, seem like unrealistic optimism. Except that the Australian Board of Control issued its invitation to the West Indies on 12 September 1929. Seventeen days later, the New York Stock Exchange crashed and nothing, not even cricket, was immune from the consequences.

1. A note on money. In the 1930s, Australia's currency was the pound. There were twenty shillings to the pound, and twelve pennies to the shilling. At the start of 1930, the value of the Australian pound was pegged to the value of sterling. Estimates of the purchasing power of the pound, in today's currency, are inexact and are complicated by the impact of the Depression, but a pound in 1930 bought somewhere between 80 and 100 times as much as it does today.

By 1929, Learie Constantine was the most dynamic all-round cricketer in the world.

2

Selecting a team

The members of the West Indies Cricket Board of Control assembled in Kingston, in the first week of April 1930, intending to watch the final Test match against the touring English side, before selecting the first West Indies team to visit Australia. They ended up spending much more time in Kingston than they had expected. As the series was deadlocked at one win apiece, the Test match was supposed to be played to a finish, and England soaked up most of the first three days compiling a ridiculously monumental first innings of 849, to which Andrew Sandham contributed the first Test match triple-century. The tall scoring was partly explained by an unforgiving pitch, and partly by the fact that the West Indies had left out its two best bowlers, Learie Constantine and George Francis, because they were professionals, and the Board of Control was unwilling to pay their fees. Although England claimed a first-innings lead of 563, its captain, Freddie Calthorpe, declined to enforce the follow-on, arguing that time was irrelevant, that sooner or later the pitch would begin to deteriorate, and that he didn't want to be batting when it did. Chasing a target of 836 to win the game and the series, West Indies had reached 408 for five when torrential rain prevented any further play before the time came for the English team to sail for home. The game was finally abandoned nine days after it had begun, which at least gave the selectors plenty of time to contemplate the players' form.

By 1930, cricket was played in the West Indies by men of all races and colours; but its controlling bodies were composed, still, of well-to-do white amateurs. Barbados was represented on the Board by Francis Austin, whose better-known brother, Harold, had just resigned as its president. His successor was to be the former Barbados wicket-keeper, Laurie Yearwood, who was attending the meeting on behalf of the Leeward Islands. Joseph Scheult, a bank manager and former soccer player, represented Trinidad; the Jamaican delegate was Major George

Cox, the Clerk of Public Works and captain of the Melbourne Cricket Club. PJ O'Leary Bradbury, who had opened the batting for Antigua in the 1890s, came from the Windward Islands, but British Guiana could not be bothered sending a representative, instead delegating its position to Harry Mallett. Mallett, a walking, breathing conflict of interest, was in Kingston because he was also the manager of the touring MCC team – a role which did nothing to prevent him from sitting down to select the next West Indies side.

Most selection panels include at least some members with experience of playing the game to a high standard. Not this one. Laurie Yearwood had scored only twenty first-class runs, but that was twelve more than Harry Mallett; Francis Austin had a first-class batting average of 2.08 (although, in fairness, he did take some wickets). Not one of its members had played international cricket; those who had played a little first-class cricket had done so many years earlier; and none of them had any experience of playing cricket in Australia. The Board invited the cricket authorities in each colony to submit to a list of candidates to the selectors, but those lists only emphasised that not every selector had seen every candidate in action.

Even so, it's arguable that this deeply imperfect panel was an improvement on the ones that had just selected the teams for the four Tests against England. In each game of that series, the host authority in each colony had appointed an entirely local selection committee – with predictable results. Each of the four teams had a different captain, a local man in every case. The Trinidad selectors loaded up the West Indies team with seven players from Trinidad, while no fewer than eight Jamaicans played in Kingston. There was, of course, plenty of home-town bias involved in those choices, but there were practical issues to consider as well. Jamaica, for example, is more than one thousand miles from Barbados and British Guiana, and it was not always easy for cricketers to obtain leave from work for a time-consuming journey and match. The pragmatic benefit of selecting local players was that you could be reasonably sure that they'd turn up. The result was that, altogether, 27 players were used in the four Tests.

The tour selectors began by choosing the captain. And the first thing they did was eliminate from contention the incumbent, Karl Nunes.

There was nothing wrong with Nunes' form with the bat; in the Kingston Test, he had batted for five and a half hours while compiling scores of 66 and 92. Having led the West Indies in England in 1928, he also had captaincy experience. But it wasn't good experience. He turned out to be deeply unpopular with his own team, who found him to be 'gloomy, snobbish and over-reserved' – or, as George Headley put it, 'captain was one way, and men another'. Several players had said that they were not prepared to tour again with Nunes at the helm. A solicitor with a busy legal practice, Nunes responded to the criticism by refusing all further invitations to play outside Jamaica. All in all, there was nothing to be gained by inviting him to tour Australia.

But if not Nunes, who? There was a concerted push, mostly but not only from Barbados, for the claims of Teddy Hoad. A tall, right-handed batsman with a sound technique and a neat moustache, Hoad had batted fairly well in England in 1928, although he did little in the Tests. When the MCC team played Barbados in January 1930, Hoad played an excellent innings of 147, which earned him the captaincy of the team that played in the first Test the following week. Hoad scored only 24 and 0 in the Test, and was unavailable for the rest of the series, but his reputation remained high. He was, probably, the selectors' first choice for the captaincy. But he was also the manager of a sugar plantation, for which the early months of the year were peak season. The Board of Control sent Hoad a cable asking whether he would be available to tour Australia. He replied that he was – except that he needed to be back in Barbados by the end of January. So the search for a captain continued.

No serious consideration appears to have been given to Maurice Fernandes, who had captained the West Indies in its first Test match victory, at Georgetown. Fernandes was a sound, if unexciting, player but he hadn't made many runs in his three matches against the English tourists, and had failed on the 1928 tour to England. At the age of 33, he was unlikely to improve as a batsman. He was also a modest, rather quiet, man – not at all an obvious leader.

A suggestion came from Trinidad: how about Jack Grant? The

body that governed Trinidad cricket was the Queen's Park Club, and the secretary of the Queen's Park Club was Freddie Grant, a former captain of Trinidad. Two years later, Freddie Grant would be appointed President of the Board of Control, but he was also Jack's brother – so the nomination hardly came from a disinterested source. The Trinidad Sporting Chronicle didn't think much of the idea, complaining that a 'more preposterous proposition to advance, speaking for the West Indies viewpoint, it is difficult to conjecture' and insisting that 'such a statement can only be conceived by an aberrated brain, one that needs attention when taking asylum in some sanitorium or other institution for persons demented or otherwise mentally or physically deranged… It were better that the tour be scrapped entirely than assemble an apology for a side and erroneously name it a West Indies side.'

The problem – or, at any rate, part of the problem – was that Jack Grant had never played cricket for Trinidad, and had not even lived in the West Indies for almost five years. His father, Thomas Geddes Grant, had established a trading company in Trinidad that made him an extremely wealthy man (after which he discovered oil on one of his cocoa estates, which made him wealthier still). George Copeland Grant and his twin sister, Janet, were known in their family as Jack and Jill, and the nicknames stuck. Jack and Jill were the eighth and ninth children born to Thomas' wife Christina; the tenth was Rolph, who would eventually succeed his brother as captain of the West Indies cricket team. Jack was an outstanding schoolboy cricketer at Queen's Royal College in Port of Spain. There he was taught by CLR James (who had not yet emerged as an influential socialist thinker), captained the school in soccer, and broke every one of the school's records as a batsman. But as soon as he left school, he was sent to Dalhousie University in Canada for a year, and then on to Cambridge University. There he quickly won a Blue for soccer, but it took longer for his cricket to develop. In his first two years at Cambridge, Grant was scarcely required at all by the University side (which was strong, including future internationals Maurice Turnbull, Duleepsinhji, Maurice Allom and Walter Robins). He made only a single first-class appearance for the University in his second year, batting ninth and scoring five not out against Northamptonshire. He was more successful in 1929, defying a strong Yorkshire attack to score 45 and 88 in his first appearance of the season. He couldn't quite duplicate that form in the games that followed, and an effort to turn him into an all-rounder was doomed to failure, but he earned his Blue and ended the season with 691 runs at an average of 31.40. His batting had been unexciting, but workmanlike and tenacious. It was important, he believed, that he had scored runs against Yorkshire, because he heard that Wilfred Rhodes spoke highly of him when he toured the West Indies at the end of the season.

Those were his credentials for the captaincy of the West Indies: one modestly successful season for Cambridge, lots of runs for Queen's Royal College, and a little praise from Wilfred Rhodes. He had never been captain of any team of adults. He did not know any of the leading West Indian players. It was not even certain that he would return to the West Indies after the tour – he was due to be married to Ida Russell, the daughter of the Chief Justice of Southern Rhodesia, where it seemed likely that he'd settle. But Harry Mallett was enthusiastic about him. 'The West Indies would be lucky', Mallett gushed, 'if they got Grant to captain the side.' What secured the captaincy for Grant was the fact that he seemed like the right sort of chap for the job: a Cambridge man from a wealthy family would be well-equipped to handle the social occasions and speech-making that were then an unavoidable part of a touring captain's role.

And, of course, as Grant himself later acknowledged, 'it could not be disputed that my white colour was a major factor a major factor in my being given this post.' West Indian cricket was still governed by white men who were not yet ready to accept a black man in a position of leadership. The obvious choice for the captaincy was Learie Constantine, the dynamic all-rounder who was the first man chosen in the side and an astute thinker about the game. But not only was Constantine black, he was also a professional cricketer, having signed a Lancashire League contract with Nelson in 1929. West Indian cricket shared with England and Australia the belief that professionals ought not to act as captains. Constantine came to respect Grant personally, but pointed out that he 'went straight from Cambridge across the Pacific. It is no disparagement of him to say that whatever they taught him at Cambridge, it could not have been our respective merits as parts of a team, because the same might have been said of anyone else who was as new to us as he was.... Until players and captains are considered on their merits by a justice blind to the colour of their skins, the West Indies will never take a place in Test Match cricket commensurate with the skill of individual West Indian exponents.'

But that time was still distant, and so, almost by default, the captaincy was offered to Jack Grant. The Board of Control announced its captain on 13 April, three days before naming the other fifteen players. After Grant, the first batsman chosen was George Headley, the compact young Jamaican who had performed so brilliantly against the Englishmen. In his first Test, he scored 21 and 176; after failing in Trinidad, he scored 112 and 114 at Georgetown, and in the final match he compiled a monumental 223. Remarkably, he did all this at the age of twenty. The English team was far from representative – many leading players stayed home, besides which an entirely separate team also styled as England was playing Tests in New Zealand at much the same time. But it fielded a decent attack, led by veteran spinner Wilfred Rhodes and the lively young fast bowler Bill Voce. Headley mastered them all. He had a solid technique, a wide range of strokes, a calm temperament and a powerful appetite for runs. Within the space of a few months, he had emerged as not only the best batsman in the West Indies, but also one of the finest in the world. The only other batsman to have played all four Tests of the series against England was Clifford Roach, a tall and stylish opening batsman from Barbados. Roach's 122 in Bridgetown was the first Test century scored for the West Indies; in the third Test, at Georgetown, he added the first double-century. Roach, a solicitor from Port of Spain, was an attacking stroke player, a brilliant fieldsman and an automatic choice for the tour.

After Grant, Headley and Roach, the batting selections became more difficult. The selectors were keen to pick Frank Martin, a left-hander from Jamaica, who had performed well in England in 1928. But there were concerns about his availability: Martin was the cashier of the United Fruit

Company, and he took his work extremely seriously. It was said that when Jamaica played matches in Kingston, Martin would bat at four or six in the order so that he could remain at his office until lunchtime, although there were times when he was summoned from his desk by an urgent phone call after the unexpected fall of early wickets. Martin had been unavailable for all the Tests against England except for the last, in Kingston. But the United Fruit Company (which also employed George Headley as a clerk) happily granted him leave, and he was added to the team. Martin was almost 37 years old, although for cricketing purposes he usually knocked two years from his age. Quiet and self-effacing, he was a solid, reliable presence at the top of the order, especially efficient through the on side.

Frank de Caires had played three Tests against England, making an immediate impact in Bridgetown with scores of 80 and 70. He was a tall right-hander, still aged no more than twenty, who often started hesitantly but could drive and cut with terrific power through the off side. His prosperous family, of Portuguese descent, owned a trading company in Demerara, and he had been educated at Stonyhurst College, a Jesuit school in Lancashire. There he spent four years in the first eleven, although he was overshadowed by his younger brother, Herman, who was seen as the better prospect. Herman, an all-rounder who represented the Young Amateurs at Lord's in 1928, was often spoken of as the best cricketer ever to pass through Stonyhurst, and was also an excellent Rugby player – but he was lost to West Indies cricket (except, decades later, as a commentator on radio) when he decided to remain in England and join the Jesuit order. Frank, on his return to British Guiana, developed his batting so rapidly that, not much more than a year after leaving school, he hit 133 against Trinidad in his third first-class match. He was a notoriously slow and clumsy fieldsman, but he had done enough with the bat to win a spot in the touring party. At the conclusion of the Kingston Test, he returned home to Georgetown by air, taking what he called 'my first flip in an aeroplane.'

To that core of five batsmen, the selectors added three men who had taken no part at all in the series against England. Lionel Birkett owed his place to a massive innings of 253 for Trinidad against British Guiana in October 1929. Originally from Barbados, Birkett had moved to Trinidad to study at the College of Tropical Agriculture. He was employed as an industrial chemist in the sugar industry, and his work had prevented him from playing any matches against the tourists. But the estate on which he worked was owned by his new captain's brother, Freddie Grant, who was happy to grant him leave to visit Australia. A well-organised, tall right-hander, he was named as Jack Grant's vice-captain, although his previous experience of captaincy had been leading his school team, Harrison College, against Grant's Queen's Royal College. 'Barto' Bartlett, a solicitor's clerk, had first played for Barbados before his eighteenth birthday, and toured England in 1928. Except that he scored 67 for Barbados against the MCC, he had done nothing particularly noteworthy during the 1929-30 season, and hadn't appeared in any of the Tests, but he was experienced and a known quantity. At his best, he was an attractive, attacking player, especially good on the back foot.

Oscar Wight's selection is harder to understand. He had played well in the trials for the 1928 team to England, but missed selection. He had started the 1929-30 season in imperious form, cracking 75 and 103 for British Guiana against Barbados. But after one more, undistinguished, match, his season was over: he played no games against the Englishmen, and when the touring team was announced, he was not even in the West Indies, having travelled to England (either for a holiday, or on business with the successful trading company owned by his father, who was also the Mayor of Georgetown). British Guiana was effectively unrepresented on the selection committee, and it's tempting to speculate that the selectors confused him with his older brother, Vibart, who had not only toured England in 1928 but also played in the Georgetown Test against England. At his best, Oscar Wight was a forceful, aggressive player, but he had played very little serious cricket. Like Frank de Caires, Wight had been to an English public school.

Clifford Roach and Edwin St Hill

From left to right: George Headley, J Derek Sealey and Errol Hunte.

And, like his captain, he had been to Cambridge, although not for long: he barely made it through his first term (the Michaelmas Term of 1924) before returning home.

If there was any batsman who was unlucky to be omitted, it was Clarence Passailaigue. Passailaigue was a remarkably versatile sportsman, a prominent tennis player and useful sprinter, who was also considered the finest goalkeeper ever to play for the Jamaican national soccer team. Apparently because Karl Nunes did not rate his batting highly, he was 28 years old before he was selected to make his debut in first-class cricket, against MCC in the colony match just before the Kingston Test. Going to the crease at 123 for four, with Jamaica trailing far behind MCC's 396, he hammered 183 in rapid time. That performance earned him selection for the Test, in which he hit a careful 44 in the first innings and was unbeaten on two when the game ended. He was a brilliant fieldsman, and had better recent form than Oscar Wight. But he also had a remarkable fondness for the sweep shot – he played it so often, and hit it so hard, that his team-mates called him 'The Broom' – and the selectors appear to have been suspicious of his methods. Nor did it help his cause that the selectors took advice from Karl Nunes. In his next first-class match, in 1931-32, against a team assembled by Lord Tennyson that included five Test match bowlers, Passailaigue hit 261 not out in just over four hours. He shared an unbroken partnership of 487 with George Headley (which was and remains the world record for the sixth wicket). So in his first three first-class matches he hit 490 runs and averaged 245, but his first Test match turned out also to be the last of a truly inexplicable career.

The frontline bowlers selected themselves. The selection committee expected Australian pitches to be hard, bouncy and fast, so the attack was based on pace. Learie Constantine was genuinely fast when he extended himself, and made effective use of a disconcerting bouncer – although he could also operate, with great variety, at a slower pace. He was a versatile, aggressive bowler – besides which, he was a devastating attacking batsman, and perhaps the best all-round fieldsman in the world. He would be supported by Herman Griffith and George Francis. Griffith, a sanitation inspector from Barbados, was 36 years old and past his best. But while he had lost a little of his pace, he could bowl long spells without flagging or losing his length, and he attacked the off stump persistently with a little bit of movement either way. His best delivery was a late outswinger, which might have been even more potent had he been supported by abler catchers in the slips. He had taken 5-63 against England at Port of Spain. George Francis of Barbados, another of the 1928 tourists to England, had played only one Test in the 1929-30 series, at Georgetown. There, his six wickets, including 4-40 in the first innings, had helped West Indies to achieve its first victory in Test cricket. Francis, who had a distinctive leap in his delivery stride, operated at much the same pace as Griffith. Unusually for a fast bowler, he was an excellent catcher in the slips. Constantine, Francis and Griffith were, potentially, a match-winning combination, and together they formed a stronger pace attack than anything Australia could assemble.

Among the slower bowlers, there were fewer options. The best in the West Indies was probably 'Snuffy' Browne, a barrister from British Guiana, who could bowl inswing with the new ball before turning to leg spin later in the innings. But after the Georgetown Test against England (in which he hit a rapid, unbeaten 70), Browne declared that he had 'played my last Test against England'. No one really understood whether this was a retirement from all international cricket, and the selectors were unsure whether he would go to Australia if invited. By the time that Browne clarified that he was available for the tour, it was too late to persuade the selectors that he was enthusiastic about it. Instead, they chose Tommy Scott and Edwin St Hill.

Tommy Scott, a tall leg spinner who could bat usefully, made his first-class debut for Jamaica against a touring MCC team in April 1911. It was a highly memorable occasion: Scott took 6-77 and 5-61, and was the last man dismissed in a tied game. Naturally, he held his place in the Jamaican team for the colony's next first-class game, against Barbados – in January 1925. The flint-hard pitches in Kingston offered him little by way of side-spin, and his most effective delivery was a high-bouncing top-spinner. Scott was 37 years old when he appeared in the marathon Kingston Test against England, but he was fit enough to send down 80 overs in the first innings and 25 in the second. He captured nine wickets in the game, although they cost him 374 runs. To this day, no bowler has conceded more runs in a single Test, yet this cheerful cricketer somehow emerged from the game with his reputation enhanced. He was the only specialist spinner invited to make the tour. Ellis Achong, the left-armer from Trinidad, had played a single Test against England without doing anything very memorable – and besides, he played on matting pitches in Trinidad, so his ability on turf pitches had not been well tested. There were people in Jamaica who pressed for the selection of the left-armer, George Gladstone Morais, but his experience of the Kingston Test had been even more brutal than Scott's – his only wicket cost him 189 runs. Achong and Morais stayed at home, and instead the selectors consoled themselves with the thought that Frank Martin occasionally tossed down a few overs of left-arm finger spin, and George Headley could sometimes bowl leg-breaks.

The last of the bowlers was Edwin St Hill, whose gifted brother Wilton had played three Tests for the West Indies as a batsman. Edwin was rewarded for an exceptional performance for Trinidad against British Guiana, in which he took ten wickets and scored 67. In two Tests against England, he had done nothing exceptional, but confirmed his ability to bowl long, containing spells at just above medium pace. If Grant needed a workhorse to tie up an end while the fast bowlers rested, St Hill could do that job. His half-century against British Guiana earned him an entirely undeserved reputation as an all-rounder: he never again scored any meaningful runs.

To round off the team, the selectors named three wicket-keepers, but without choosing either of the two men who were generally acknowledged as the best in the West Indies. There were still people in Trinidad who spoke in an almost mystical tone of the legendary skills of a stumper named Piggott, but Piggott was no longer young and had personal idiosyncrasies that had kept him out of the colonial team for years. Instead, George Dewhurst took the gloves for Trinidad. Dewhurst, who had toured England with the West Indies in 1923, was an outstanding gloveman, but by now his age – he was 35 – counted against him, as did the fact that the Board of Control had neither forgotten nor forgiven his reluctance to make the 1928 tour to England.

So another Trinidad man, Errol Hunte, had kept wicket in the first three Tests against England, doing an inelegant but effective job as well as scoring two stubborn half-centuries. He had been displaced for the final match by the home-town choice, Jamaica's Ivan Barrow, a decision that was greeted with dismay in Trinidad. The *Sporting Chronicle* reported Learie

Constantine as saying that he had played only once with Barrow, and found that he was "*no stumper at all. With the help of one of my colleagues, I ascertained that he stood back 17 paces from the wicket to my bowling and also to that of Francis. And even then, he was such a green horn at the job that he was unable to anticipate the strokes batsmen would make and to be able to follow the flight of the balls when I swung them so as to get in the correct position to take them. On one occasion, Sandham touched a swinger of mine, which found Barrow shaped up on the leg side whilst the ball travelled on the off side for 4 runs. On another occasion, a delivery tipped by the same batsman struck him full on the lower portion of his pads. Even to Small, Barrow failed to stand close to the wicket as do all other stumpers in taking deliveries from this bowler. Except Barrow has progressed beyond recognition (and this is unlikely since he did not have to negotiate the pace of Francis, Griffith and myself) I do not imagine he can oust any of the players of the Southern colonies.*"

Those comments prompted a strong reaction in Jamaica, one journalist insisting that Constantine was no longer welcome in that colony. As it happened, Barrow (who was only nineteen years old) made none of the 1,815 runs that were scored in the Fourth Test, but committed few errors behind the stumps, and he was named in the touring party. So were Hunte and Derek Sealy, a schoolboy from Barbados who batted brightly, bowled medium pace and kept wicket when needed. Sealy had been only 17 years and 122 days old when he made his Test debut in Bridgetown – which made him the youngest player ever to have appeared in Test cricket to that point – and he marked his first day in international cricket with a sparkling innings of 58. He was an exciting, versatile talent, and nobody complained when he was selected to tour Australia.

The touring party was completed by the inevitable Harry Mallett, as manager, with Joseph Scheult as assistant manager. Scheult, a 48 year-old manager with the Agricultural Bank in Trinidad, was also to serve as treasurer. Anywhere in Trinidad where a committee of white men gathered, there you'd find Joe Scheult – he helped to run, among other things, the Union Club, and the Football Association, and the Queen's Park Cricket Club. An observant Catholic, he also found the time to sire ten children. Having named the team's officials, the members of the Board of Control were satisfied that their task was complete. They never appreciated how close they came to needing to rethink their choice of captain.

Jack Grant was in Cambridge when he received the telegram inviting him to accept the leadership of the West Indies cricket team. He had graduated in 1929, plodding his way to a rather undistinguished third-class degree in History, but had stayed on for another year to undertake a teaching diploma. The offer of the captaincy, he knew, was an 'exceptional honour', but it also unsettled him. He and Ida Russell had just decided to marry, and the invitation to tour Australia threw their plans into disarray. 'I nearly declined the honour', Grant later reflected. The trouble was that he and Ida 'were beginning to think no longer only of what we wanted to do or what others wanted us to do, but what our Lord would have us do. We spent a month and more literally agonising over this question. It seemed insoluble. Worse still, this apparent insolubility seemed to drive a wedge between Ida and me. So deep did this wedge go that it was on the point of splitting our engagement asunder. We were a distraught and unhappy pair.'

Jack Grant's grandparents had arrived in Trinidad as Presbyterian missionaries; he had been raised in the church and never left it. He met Ida through Cambridge's Student Christian Movement, where they sang together in a choir. So Grant decided to 'give my life and problems to God in total surrender and trust and wait for the answer'. That answer turned out to be something of a compromise: the Almighty's opinion on the West Indian captaincy appears to have been that Grant should accept it, so Ida agreed to visit Jack in Trinidad when the university year ended, after which Grant would tour Australia before joining Ida in Southern Rhodesia. This was not usually how questions of Test captaincy were decided, but Jack Grant was not in any way a usual Test captain.

3

October

Two cricket teams, an opera singer and a pilot head for Australia; construction continues on the Sydney Harbour Bridge; New South Wales goes to the polls; and an arrest is made in Melbourne.

On the first day of October 1930, the first vertical hanger was suspended from the arch of the Sydney Harbour Bridge. The bridge's massive central arch, 1,654 feet long and 440 feet above the waterline at its summit, had been completed in late August. Now began the task of constructing the deck of the bridge, which was suspended from the arch by steel hangers and constructed outwards from the centre. The longest of the hangers was 192 feet long; each one needed to be lifted into place by two cranes, and then bolted to the underside of the arch.

The Harbour Bridge was the grand project of John Bradfield, the chief engineer for metropolitan railway construction in New South Wales. Bradfield had conducted a tender process in 1924, in which the successful proponent was the English firm, Dorman, Long and Co. Dorman Long began work the following year, although it wasn't until 1928 that they began to build the arch. Two massive construction worksheds were established at Milson's Point, at the northern end of the bridge, mostly for steel fabrication, and these provided employment for hundreds of boilermakers, ironworkers and riveters.

The bridge was designed to accommodate four lanes of traffic, four railway lines and two pedestrian pathways: when Sydneysiders called their bridge the largest in the world, they were referring to width, not length. But it's also the tallest bridge of its kind in the world. Sydney in 1930 was a squat city of low-rise buildings, and its new bridge soared high above everything else in sight.

§

Jack Grant prepared for the tour by spending five weeks in Trinidad in September and October, with Ida (and her mother, as chaperone), interrupting their time together to take 'regular cricket practice in the nets

The first cables are suspended from the arch of the Sydney Harbour Bridge, October 1930.

The Sydney Harbour Bridge being decked, November 1930.

with the Trinidad members of the team', and to deliver equally regular sermons in the two churches he attended.

§

The last remaining members of the Australian cricket team left England on 2 October 1930. Bert Oldfield, Ted a'Beckett, Alec Hurwood and Archie Jackson boarded a train at Victoria Station, on their way to Toulon, where they were to join the rest of their team-mates on the SS Oronsay, bound for Melbourne. They had been travelling for seven exhausting months, but the tour had been a triumph. Before the tour began, it was generally assumed that England would win the Tests comfortably, and the hosts had little trouble in taking the first of them, at Nottingham. But that was the only game the Australians lost in England, and they regained the Ashes with crushing victories at Lord's and the Oval.

This was the tour on which Donald Bradman from Bowral became, definitively, *Bradman*: the outstanding cricketer of his time – and, arguably, of any time. When the tour opened, he had been regarded as just one good prospect among a fine crop of Australian batsmen. Although there was abundant evidence of his unusual appetite for scoring runs, there were critics who pointed out that he wasn't as stylish as Archie Jackson, as charming as Alan Kippax or as exciting as Stan McCabe. Nor was he as consistently prolific as Bill Ponsford. It was true that, by scoring 452 not out against Queensland, Bradman had broken the world record for the highest score in first-class cricket, but Ponsford had already done that twice. And there were murmurs that Bradman's methods were unsuited to England's slower, softer pitches.

Bradman opened the tour by hitting 236 at Worcester, and added 185 not out against Leicestershire in his next match. On his first visit to the Oval, he scored 252 against Surrey. On the last day of May, the Australians began their match against Hampshire with Bradman still needing 46 runs to pass 1000 before the month ended. Hampshire batted first, but collapsed to Clarrie Grimmett and left the Australians about an hour to bat. Bradman, opening the innings, was 47 not out at stumps; when play resumed, he carried on to make 191. He was every bit as dominant when the Tests began. At Nottingham, he made 131, followed by 254 at Lord's. At Leeds, he scored 334, making 309 on the first day of the game. He rounded off the series with 232 at the Oval, where Australia emphatically regained the Ashes. No one had ever scored as many as his 974 runs in the series, and no-one has ever matched it since. No one had ever made so many runs, so quickly and efficiently. Playing a game in which most batsmen fail most of the time, he seemed to have inverted the odds – it was a sensation when he made a low score, because now he was expected to succeed.

Learie Constantine had watched Bradman's progress in England in 1930. 'I saw Don Bradman play his great innings at Headingly', he told an interviewer, 'and it was a revelation. I have never seen that type of batsmanship previously. He impressed me as a defensive player who can score faster than any of the so-called hurricane hitters. I should like to bowl at Bradman, not that I think I should ever get him out, but just as an experience and education.'

The Ashes tour was less successful for Archie Jackson. *Wisden* called him a 'disappointment'. He scored over a thousand runs, which was the benchmark of an acceptable English season, but was thoroughly overshadowed by Bradman and played only one significant innings in the Tests. Arthur Mailey, the former Test spinner who played alongside Jackson at the Balmain club and covered the tour as a journalist, argued that Jackson had 'failed as a rungetter, but not as a batsman. He made excellent strokes, but did not get the scores in keeping with his Australian reputation.' Jackson, he insisted, 'was nothing if not artistic and graceful'. But now, thanks largely to Bradman, cricket had a new economy which priced results above style and placed a premium on runs in bulk. Archie Jackson had some ground to make up.

§

The cricketers weren't the only Australians sailing home in triumph. On 9 October, the great soprano Dame Nellie Melba embarked on the RMS Cathay, bound for Melbourne. She was fresh from singing at a charity event in London in June, which had been billed as her final performance – although that came with no guarantee, since Melba (who was now aged sixty-nine) had been playing farewell concerts for over a decade.

Melba was revered by thousands of Australians who cared nothing at all for opera. When she toured her own country, to great acclaim, she was always careful to include several popular tunes in her repertoire, rather than bombarding her audiences with unfamiliar Italian arias. Australians might not have been able to tell Puccini from Rossini, but they knew that Melba had been born Helen Porter Mitchell in unpretentious suburban Melbourne, yet somehow became a *prima donna* at Covent Garden, the Paris Opera and the Metropolitan Opera in New York. It wasn't just that a woman from a modest background had succeeded so spectacularly – what really appealed was that she had succeeded at a refined, artistic pursuit that many people had assumed to be beyond the reach of a mere Australian. She was a walking answer to the complaint that Australians lacked culture, a one-woman exercise in national self-validation.

§

Tremendous excitement was generated in Melbourne by the capture of the State's most wanted criminal, Richard Buckley. Buckley, who was 67 years old, stood accused of the murder of bank manager Thomas Berriman – in 1923. He'd eluded the police for seven years, in which time he'd been given the nickname, 'The Grey Ghost'.

Buckley was first imprisoned for assault when he was fifteen years old. He had learned shoemaking as a trade, but his true talent was for the insouciant performance of acts of appalling violence. That knack made him a valued associate of the notorious psychopath 'Squizzy' Taylor, a hoodlum who dominated Melbourne's criminal underworld in the 1920s. Buckley assisted Taylor in a string of armed robberies, which typically ended with Buckley being captured while Taylor escaped. Having served time for 'shooting with intent to kill' during a robbery at Melbourne's Trades Hall, Buckley was released just in time to join Taylor on another job.

Taylor had somehow learned that Thomas Berriman, the manager of the Glenferrie branch of the Commercial Bank, caught the eleven o'clock train to the city each morning, carrying a briefcase bulging with cash. Berriman always did this unaccompanied and, although he carried a revolver in his pocket, it was difficult to imagine an easier target. Taylor didn't take part in the robbery itself – instead, he sent Buckley and a petty crook (and bigamist) named Angus Murray. At precisely eleven o'clock on the day of the robbery, Taylor went to loiter conspicuously outside the Russell Street Police Station, amusing himself at the thought that the police themselves would furnish him with his alibi.

The robbery was botched. Berriman offered more resistance than Taylor had expected, and Buckley shot him in the chest. He lived for two days, long enough to identify Murray and Buckley from police photographs. Murray was caught, tried and hanged. But Buckley remained in hiding. There were rumours that he'd fled the country, that he'd been seen somewhere in America, but in fact he never left Melbourne.

The hero of the hour was Detective Fred Lacey, who was said to have a gift for 'shadowing' criminals. He did this mostly by disguising himself as a woman, while a colleague, Detective Bill Coffey, posed as his boyfriend. 'His make-up as a woman is said to be excellent', one newspaper reported, 'and though Buckley's friends at times had a suspicion the police were on his trail, never once was Lacey's disguise suspected' while he and Coffey 'drove in a car through the haunts of the underworld with death in close vicinity.' No one ever really explained why Lacey needed to dress as a woman to do this, and it seems never to have occurred to the police that whatever Lacey was doing in drag could have been done much more efficiently by an actual woman.

Lacey was coy about how he came to learn where Buckley was hiding, saying only that 'after many days of shadowing, I was able to strike a clue'. What seems to have happened is that Buckley had been living on regular allowances from a criminal associate, who tipped off the police when he tired of making the payments. In any event, Buckley was caught by surprise when Lacey led a squad of detectives into the house in Bowen Street, Moonee Ponds, where he had been hiding. It later emerged that Buckley's granddaughter had been visiting the house on a regular basis, a rather pertinent potential clue that had eluded Lacey, who

The 1930 Australian Cricket team in England, photographed by Bolland.

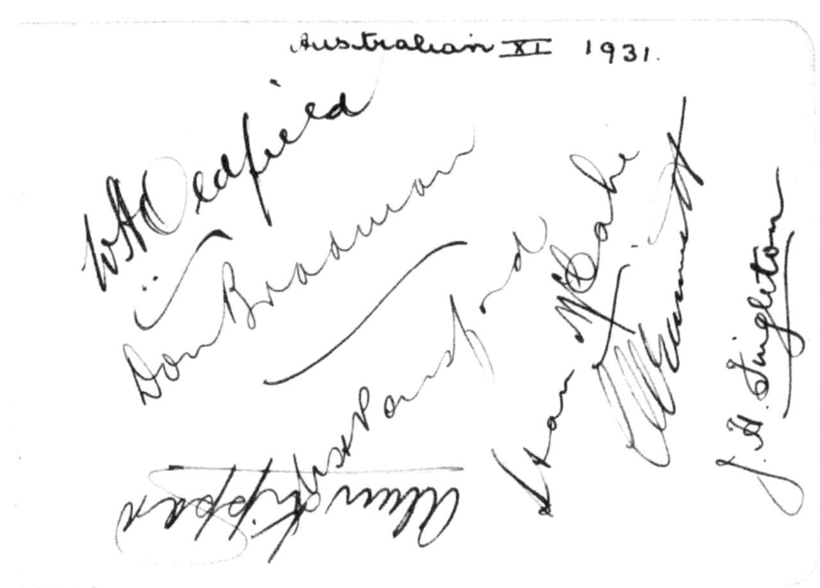

had been too busy dressing as a woman in gangland haunts. Anyway, Lacey wasn't the only master of disguise involved in the incident: the police issued a statement explaining that it had taken seven years to find Buckley because he had 'completely altered his appearance' – by growing a beard.

§

The West Indies team assembled at Colon, in Panama, on 21 October. This was a mistake.

The Board of Control had originally planned for the touring party to sail from Panama on a steamer belonging to the New Zealand Trading & Shipping Company, departing on 9 October. Unfortunately, by the time the Board got around to making bookings, there were no berths left on the vessel and the next available ship, the S.S. *Tamaroa,* sailed on 23 October. That meant that the West Indians were now due to arrive in Sydney on 18 November, only three days before playing their first game – against a powerful New South Wales team. It left the team with disturbingly little time in which to acclimatise and practice. To compensate, the West Indies Board accepted an invitation to play a two-day match against Wellington when the team stopped in New Zealand to change ships.

Blazers, ties, caps and jumpers – which had arrived from a London tailor – were distributed to the West Indian players. For almost a century, people have spoken of the 'maroon' West Indian cap, but the official description of the colours was 'deep burgundy with a green and silver trim'. It's unclear why West Indies teams used these colours when touring – at home, they played in navy blue caps. The team also acquired a large banner featuring the West Indies badge (a palm tree rising from a tiny island) on a burgundy background. This curious flag – designed by no-one remembers whom to represent a country that never was – would be flown at every ground where the West Indians played.

George Headley particularly enjoyed his few days in Panama, where he had been born, and where he had spent the first eight years of his life. 'How thrilled I was', he wrote, 'at this opportunity, as I never believed I would see Panama again.' An exhibition match had been planned, to entertain the large expatriate West Indian community, but it was delayed by heavy rain and began only after the local groundsman poured kerosene on the pitch and set it alight in an attempt to dry it out. What followed, Headley recalled, was 'a most enjoyable game, playing as cricket of that type should be played. Learie Constantine delighted the crowd with some of his brilliant and clean hitting. I remember well that he had four sixes in one over; but that is like Learie when he gets cracking. I made 34 runs before being caught, but Oh! How I would have loved to have made a century in the land of my birth.' There may not have been time for that anyway: more rain washed out the game shortly after his dismissal.

Immediately after their match, the players attended a dinner in their honour, and then went directly to the Tamaroa, which sailed at midnight.

§

Unquestionably, Don Bradman was Australia's most popular sporting hero. His closest competition came from a four-year-old New Zealander.

Phar Lap was a chestnut gelding, who was spotted by Sydney trainer Harry Telford at yearling sales on the South Island in 1928. Telford persuaded an American businessman, David Davis, to let him bid for the horse, which was sold for 160 guineas. When Telford returned to Australia with the colt, Davis was so unimpressed by Phar Lap's scrawny appearance that he refused to pay Telford to train him. Eventually the two men hammered out an agreement under which Telford leased Phar Lap from Davis, took responsibility for his training, and kept two-thirds of any winnings. Phar Lap began racing as a two-year-old in February 1929, finishing last in a field of thirteen in the Randwick Nursery Handicap. He finished out of the money in his next three races, too, which seemed to vindicate Davis' judgment. But at the AJC Spring Carnival at Randwick, something extraordinary happened. The unfancied, gangly galloper won three races in succession. He was taken to Melbourne, where he won the Derby and finished third in the Melbourne Cup (won by another New Zealand horse, Nightmarch, who was by the same sire as Phar Lap, Night Raid). Then he finished the season by winning nine consecutive events. Within a year, Phar Lap had transformed into 'the wonder horse'.

No-one had known who Phar Lap was when he arrived at the Sydney Spring Carnival in October 1929. A year later, at the same meeting, he was impossible to back – he entered three events, was priced at 10 to 1 on in each race, and won all three, beating Nightmarch each time. Phar Lap won the

Phar Lap, withb strapper Tommy Woodcock.

Spring Stakes as if it were 'an exercise gallop', jockey Jim Pike pulling him up well before the finish. He put in a more serious effort in the Craven Plate, beating Nightmarch by six lengths and setting, or so it was said, a new Australian record over ten furlongs. And on the last day of the meeting, he trotted through to win the Randwick Plate without extending himself at all. Nightmarch's owner decided that there was no point trying to repeat his horse's success in the Melbourne Cup, and shipped him back to New Zealand, where he could find races that Phar Lap wouldn't enter. But Phar Lap's success was a mixed blessing for the sport. The Australian Jockey Club reported that betting on its Spring Carnival had dropped by almost fifty percent from the previous year. Partly this was a result of the Depression, but it was also Phar Lap's fault: nobody with any sense backed him to lose, and it simply wasn't worthwhile backing him to win. One hopeful punter at Randwick tried to place a bet of £1,090 on Phar Lap, which would have returned just £109, only to be told by the bookie, 'I'm not giving my money away'.

§

Money was, however, given away to Archie Jackson. Possibly. As Jackson sailed home, the newspapers reported that he had received a large legacy from a relative overseas. The details were garbled. Some reports insisted that he had been left £2,000, others said it was only £1,000. In some reports the benefactor was Archie's grandfather (his mother's father had, in fact, died in Scotland in 1929), while according to others, it was a wealthy uncle who had made his fortune in America. Or Africa. Most reports agreed that the trustees of the estate had been unable to identify or locate Jackson until he turned up in Scotland with the Australian cricket team. Quizzed by the press, Jackson's mother said that she had received a letter and a telegram from her son concerning the legacy, that he would explain it all when he got home, and that she understood that she was the beneficiary named in the will. No one seems to know whether the Jacksons ever actually received anything at all.

§

The Shaw, Savill & Albion Company, owners of the *Tamaroa*, instructed the West Indies cricket team that 'not more than one trunk, a travelling case, and cricket bag will comprise the luggage of each player.'

§

The Sydney Harbour Bridge posed as a symbol of a dynamic, prosperous modern city. The truth was rather different. By October 1930, Sydney, like the rest of Australia, was crippled by the effects of the Great Depression.

The Depression was a global catastrophe, but it affected some countries more severely than others, and nowhere were its impacts felt more keenly than in Australia. Partly, this was because of the exceptionally high level of government debt, and that was due in large measure to Australia's involvement in the Great War. When the United Kingdom declared war on Germany in 1914, Australia not only joined the fight, but agreed to pay for it. Almost half a million men enlisted in the services, and Australia's cash reserves and tax base were far too modest to fund such a monumental enterprise, so the war effort was paid for largely by loans obtained from the Bank of England and other London banks. The Australian government ended up borrowing around £93 million to pay for its part in the war. That amount may seem unremarkable today, but the entire Commonwealth budget for 1930-31 provided for government expenditure of only £64 million – and the government had continued to borrow heavily in the years after the war, mostly to invest in extensive infrastructure projects. The heavy burden of interest payments left Australia's public finances in a weakened condition, utterly unable to resist the shocks of the Depression.

Australia's economy was heavily dependent upon its exports of wool, wheat and iron ore. By early 1930, global prices for wool and wheat had plunged so dramatically that it was impossible for Australian famers to sell their produce for more than its cost. And, since the Depression reduced global demand for steel, there was also reduced demand for iron ore. Lower demand in the Australian economy had a profound impact upon the manufacturing sector, and thousands of workers were thrown into unemployment. By October 1930, around 21% of the Australian workforce was unemployed – and that figure is undoubtedly an understatement, since the statistics only captured workers who belonged to a trade union.

There was little that James Scullin's Labor government could do to improve matters. Scullin is arguably the unluckiest politician in Australian history: he took office barely two weeks after the Wall Street Crash, walking into an utterly unmanageable crisis. He was hampered by the fact that his government controlled the House of Representatives, but not the Senate, which meant that the opposition Nationalist Party had the power to block its legislation. Scullin was torn between his instinct to stimulate economic activity through government spending, and demands from the opposition – and the English banks – to cut back the federal budget. It was an impossible balancing act. A fundamentally decent man, Scullin enjoyed simple pleasures: his idea of fun was playing violin duets with his wife, and he announced that he would not live in the Prime Minister's official residence, The Lodge, because it was an unnecessary extravagance. But he attracted intense criticism when he decided to travel to London to plead for yet another loan and attend the Imperial Conference (a regular gathering of Prime Ministers of Britain's self-governing dominions). Throughout the second half of 1930, Australia's Prime Minister was out of the country, and while he was undoubtedly working hard, it's never wise politics for a Prime Minister to be abroad during a crisis. Especially when the Prime Minister is also acting as the Treasurer. Scullin temporarily held the Treasury portfolio because 'Red Ted' Theodore, the highly talented incumbent, had been stood down from cabinet while he was under investigation for corruption. It was alleged that, during his time as Premier of Queensland, Theodore had procured the government purchase of the worthless Mungana copper mine, in which he happened to hold a financial interest. Australia was in the middle of the gravest economic crisis in its history, and it was effectively rudderless.

Cricket was not insulated from the effects of the Depression. In good times, there was a lengthy waiting list for membership of the Sydney Cricket Ground, but membership was a luxury and, as the new season opened, there were – for the first time in decades – places freely available to anyone who could afford one. The New South Wales Cricket Association announced its charges for the West Indies games in Sydney, which ranged from three shillings and sixpence for an adult in the grandstand for the Test, to ninepence for a child on the Hill in the NSW match. These were the lowest charges permitted by the agreement between the Australian Board of Control and the West Indies Board of Control, and they were also the lowest charges for a Test in Sydney for nearly twenty years. And still, the number of people who had the money to spend a day at the Test was diminishing every day.

§

The Australian cricket season was already underway, although the country's best players would not arrive home for another month. In Melbourne, the St Kilda club selected a young left-arm wrist spinner, Les Fleetwood-Smith, to make his First Grade debut. He was the team's third spinner, behind the Test veterans Bert Ironmonger and Don Blackie, and he endured a brutal initiation. Jack Ryder, now forty-one years old but still a powerful batsman, cracked 161 in rapid time for Collingwood. Fleetwood-Smith eventually took a wicket, but his 13 overs were plundered for 83 runs.

§

The first representative match of the season was the annual game between Queensland Colts and New South Wales Colts, played at the Exhibition Ground in Brisbane. This was a contest that seldom attracted all that much attention, but this time Queensland had selected a young indigenous fast bowler, Eddie Gilbert, who was said to be as quick as anyone else in Australia. In Queensland in 1930 indigenous people were subject to the Aboriginals Protection and Restriction of the Sale of Opium Act of 1897, the effect of which, so far as Gilbert was concerned, was that he was required to live at the Barambah Aboriginal Reserve, which he could leave only with the permission of the Protector of Aboriginals. Gilbert was allowed to travel to Brisbane for the Colts match only after the secretary of the Queensland Cricket Association undertook to be responsible for him during the match.

Gilbert was a small, wiry man who took only a very short approach to the bowling crease, but generated his speed through a whippy action and a distinct flick of the wrist. The New South Wales team began its innings late on the first day of the game, and Gilbert caused an immediate sensation. He took two wickets and had two catches missed, surprising the visiting batsmen with his 'amazing pace off the pitch'. He maintained his hostility on the second day, working through the innings to finish with the impressive return of 6-82. His best support came from another unusual bowler, a 19 year-old left-arm wrist spinner from the country, named Jack Pizzey.

The Queensland selectors promptly named Gilbert, but not Pizzey, in their squad for the first Sheffield Shield match of the season. There were whispers in Brisbane that he achieved his surprising pace through an illegal bowling action, but the manager of the New South Wales Colts team was untroubled. Gilbert's action, he thought, 'is quite fair, and I think that some people must be confusing the turn of the wrist with the elbow action when they say that he throws. I have no doubt whatever about his action, which I think is perfectly fair. He is a fine bowler, and he has really troubled our batsmen. We would very much like to see him in Sydney.'

In the gap between the end of the Ashes tour and the start of the Sheffield Shield, there wasn't much for cricket reporters to discuss, and Gilbert's performance attracted a great deal of attention. 'What an interesting circumstance it would be', wrote Dr Les Poidevin in the *Sydney Mail*, 'if in a Test match we could oppose the visiting West Indies team with a bowler as dark-skinned and fast in pace as their own 'express', Constantine!'

§

Two international teams were converging on Australia, the returning Ashes-winning side across the Indian Ocean, and the West Indians from over the Pacific. The voyage was a bleak experience for George Headley, 'a poor sailor', who suffered from 'awful sea sickness.' He recalled that 'for the first few days of this journey I was as sick as a dog. What made matters even worse for me was that my room-mate, Edwin St Hill, was none too good a sailor either, and so we suffered together and consoled each other. We gradually improved and were able to take a little exercise and eventually put in some cricket practice and played deck games, in an area netted off for the purpose.'

Despite Headley's discomfort, it was an easy voyage, made in what Learie Constantine called 'dreamland weather'. The games deck was reserved for the West Indies team for an hour each day, and they practised as much as they could in that cramped space. It was in these narrow nets, with a ship's deck for a pitch, that Jack Grant began the gradual process of getting to know his team mates. He was an exceptionally earnest man, who deliberated carefully before making any decision, and he realised that 'I had to know where I stood and what my attitude to race was… I needed to know what my thinking was. Even more importantly, I needed to know what was the depth of my feeling.' As he reflected, it dawned on Grant that 'my thinking was not profound and my feelings not deep. I took it for granted that we were one and I accepted my team-mates as persons and as friends.' But he also knew that 'as a white man, I had advantages which a black man was unable to have', and 'consciously or unconsciously, I was heir to certain assumptions on race that were sociological rather than theological, and passing rather than permanent. There was plenty of room to shed some racial attitudes and to grow into better ones. All in all, I had a long way to go'.

§

Australia's mania for contests and records was not confined to the cricket field and racetrack. On 22 October, thousands of people gathered at Mascot Airport to watch Wing Commander Charles Kingsford Smith arrive in the *Southern Cross Junior*. Flying solo, Kingsford Smith had just won a London to Darwin air race in a new record time – ten days (or, as Kingsford Smith insisted, nine days, 21 hours and forty minutes). This beat Bert Hinkler's old record by five and a half days. Kingsford Smith calculated that, during the race, he spent 110 hours in the air.

The *Southern Cross Junior* was an Avro Avian biplane, with a single seat, which was open to the elements, and a single, 120 horsepower, engine – which had only about two-thirds of the power of a standard motor vehicle engine today. It did have, however, a welded steel fuselage, making it slightly sturdier than the wood-and-canvas contraptions that Kingsford Smith had flown previously. He followed a carefully-planned route, which took him to Rome, Athens, Aleppo, Basra, Bandar Abbas, Karachi, Allahabad, Rangoon, Singapore, Atamboea and Darwin. Elaborate arrangements had been made by the Vacuum Oil Company to ensure that the correct fuel – 'Plume Spirit' – would be available at every stop along the way.

'The worst leg of an arduous flight', Kingsford Smith declared, 'was between Rangoon and Singapore. Terrible head-winds caused rough flying, and the weather generally was frightful. Rainstorms pelted against the machine with positive fury, and low dense cloud banks forced me to fly low into the worst of the wind.' Flying over the Alps had been no picnic either – 'it was terrifically bumpy and had I not been strapped in most certainly I would have been thrown out. The machine bucked like a wild horse and I had no spurs. That did not make me air sick, of course, but I developed a very sick feeling inside when cutting off a corner at 3500 feet. Beneath me were precipitous peaks with jagged teeth. I got into a patch so bumpy that I could not keep the engine going as the petrol would not sit in the bottom of my tank. It was too terrifying to look down in search of a probable landing place. All that I got by that was a bigger fright as bigger teeth reared up all around me.' How had

Kingsford Smith managed to cope with all these perils? Well, 'by smoking all day long. Of course', he added, 'I exercised great care in doing so.'

§

Voters in New South Wales went to the polls to elect a State government on 25 October, and handed a landslide victory to the Labor leader, Jack Lang. Lang's party won almost twice as many votes as Thomas Bavin's Nationalists (a conservative party whose guiding principle, paradoxically, was loyalty to Britain in all things). A tall, broad-shouldered man, universally known as 'The Big Fella', Lang was a powerful orator not given to understatement. 'No previous election', he thundered, 'has meant so much to the Australian people and no previous decision has been so gratifying.'

Lang had been born into an impoverished family in Sydney in 1876, and left school at the age of fourteen to enter the workforce. He became a successful estate agent in western Sydney, moved into local politics, and entered the New South Wales Parliament in 1913. He was humourless, solitary, cunning and extremely ambitious. Bert Evatt, another leading Labor figure, found it impossible to warm to Lang because he never displayed even the smallest degree of interest in any sport. Through sheer force of will, Lang became the dominant figure in New South Wales Labor, leading the party to a narrow election victory in 1925. That government failed to serve its full term, losing an early election, but not before Lang introduced a pension for widows with dependent children, a piece of legislation that many voters remembered with gratitude. Lang had no very coherent political philosophy, and was driven primarily by a will to power, rather than by any specific ethos, although he was vehemently opposed to Communism. But he had a populist's finely-tuned instinct for what voters wanted to hear. In the October 1930 election, he promised both increased public works to ease unemployment, and a balanced budget, without dwelling for too long on how that particular circle might be squared.

Lang campaigned relentlessly, travelling all over the State. He believed that his oratory was his strength, and took elaborate precautions to protect his voice. The journalist Frederick Carleton Brown reported that Lang gave up smoking during the campaign: 'His pipe was discarded a week before he delivered his policy speech and he went through the campaign without a smoke... Care of his voice was of very big concern to Mr Lang. He left nothing to chance. He travelled as much as possible in closed-in cars with the windows up, and denied himself the cool country breezes on the hottest days lest a draught might bring him a cold. He made it a cardinal rule in his travels not to speak in the open air. If a town or hamlet could not provide a hall or covered-in building, it did not hear Mr Lang.'

When a town could hear Mr Lang, it often got to listen to one of his attacks on Sir Otto Niemeyer. Niemeyer was a director of the Bank of England, who had been invited to Australia by Scullin to advise on the country's financial plight, and was still travelling around the nation. Niemeyer gave precisely the kind of advice one would expect from a lender: that Australia should pay its debts, and that to do so its governments should reduce spending. If that resulted in lower wages and a lower standard of living in Australia, Australians would simply have to become accustomed to it. He had nothing to say about how the Australian economy could be revived, apart from suggesting that the price of wool and wheat might rise eventually. Niemeyer was a perfect target for Lang's demagoguery – a representative of an oppressive foreign banker, with a suspiciously alien name. Often Lang's diatribes against Niemeyer were tinged with anti-Semitism (this puzzled Niemeyer, who pointed out that not only was he not Jewish, he didn't even like Jews). At one meeting, a heckler tried to correct Lang's pronunciation of Niemeyer's name, to which Lang replied, 'It's all the same whether it's "Nymyer", "Nemeer", "Neemeyer" or "Nightmare"!'

Australia's Constitution allocates powers and responsibilities between the Federal government and the State governments and, especially in difficult times, that system operates most efficiently when the two levels of government are broadly in sympathy with each other. Lang's election meant that the Labor Party held government at the Federal level, as well as in the two most populous states, New South Wales and Victoria. In theory, this should have made things easier for Prime Minister Scullin. But Jack Lang was not an easy man. Nor was he a team player.

§

Wellington is some 7,500 miles from Panama and, even in fine weather, the Tamaroa needed three weeks to cover that distance.

On the long journey across the Pacific, Jack Grant had plenty of time to formulate a strategy for the tour, and he soon grasped that he had been given a woefully unbalanced team. There was no way, on a sixteen-match tour, that he could keep three wicket-keepers meaningfully occupied. That meant that Derek Sealy was really in the group as a batsman, but in that case, Grant had nine batsmen competing for six spots, which felt like at least one too many. On the other hand, he had only five specialist bowlers, only one of whom was a spinner. So there would be few opportunities to rest the bowlers, and an injury to any one of them could be catastrophic.

In his report to the Board of Control at the end of the tour, Grant observed that the touring party should not have included sixteen players. But that was the wrong conclusion. What he really meant was, the touring party should not have included sixteen players *like this*.

§

On the morning of 28 October, boilermaker Roy Kelly stood on a narrow platform under the decking of the Sydney Harbour Bridge, driving rivets into the structure. It had drizzled early in the day, the surface was a little slippery, and he was wearing rubber-soled boots with imperfect grip. His foot slipped slightly, he lost his balance and he tumbled backwards into space, 170 feet above the water.

Sixteen men died while working on the construction of the bridge, but Kelly wasn't one of them. 'I tried to clutch something, but there was nothing there to clutch,' he later told a journalist, 'and down I went. I turned a somersault, and then I remembered that I must concentrate upon entering the water either head first or feet first. I waved my arms and screwed up my body in an effort to do this. I began to fall down feet first, and I almost felt satisfied. I clasped my right hand over my nose and mouth. And then I hit the water. Unfortunately I was not quite upright, otherwise I don't think that I would have been hurt at all. I did not go under very far, and it seemed only an instant from the moment I fell from the bridge to the time that I was struggling on the surface. Struggling and alive.'

A man named Reg Coombs, who was working on a nearby punt, swam out to help Kelly, only to fumble his rescue and push Kelly back under the water. But eventually he dragged Kelly to a buoy, to which the two men clung while they waited for a boat to arrive. Kelly was taken to hospital, where he was found to have suffered nothing more serious than two broken ribs and shock. He was presented with a gold watch, and a special medal struck to commemorate his survival. And then, two weeks later, he was back at work, driving in rivets.

§

When the S.S. *Oronsay*, with its cargo of Australian cricketers, reached Fremantle on 28 October, all the waiting journalists thronged to Bradman. They got nothing, except for 'I've had a good time, but I'm not talking to the press.' Bradman had signed a contract with the Fairfax newspaper group to serialise the story of his 22 year-old life, and it was a term of the agreement that he was to give nothing away for free to any of Fairfax's competitors.

Alan Fairfax.

4

November

Queensland leads in the Sheffield Shield; the West Indians arrive in Sydney, where they're robbed; Dame Nellie Melba is indisposed; and there are no surprises in the Melbourne Cup.

Queensland had been admitted to the Sheffield Shield competition in 1926-27, but it had not enjoyed an easy introduction. The State had finished last in three of its four seasons, creeping just above South Australia in 1928-29. The 1929-30 season had been a disaster: with five outright defeats and a loss on the first innings, Queensland had mustered only a single competition point (out of a possible 30) from its six games.

Yet in the first week of November 1930, Queensland sat proudly at the top of the competition table, having thoroughly outplayed South Australia. Most of the credit went to 'Mo' Biggs, who scored the only century of his career, and the vastly experienced Cecil Thompson, who compiled 78, while quick bowler 'Pud' Thurlow's 5-25 helped to rout the visitors for just 72 in their first innings. It also helped that Eddie Gilbert's impact was immediate. In his opening spell, he worked up a lively pace and repeatedly hit the pads of opener Gordon Harris. Frank Gough, the Queensland captain, gave him a short rest, and then brought him back into the attack to bowl to Laurence Walsh and Bert Tobin. A good-length ball beat Walsh's hopeful lunge and bowled him; moments later, Tobin was far too late coming down on a yorker, and he lost his stumps as well. Gilbert took two more wickets in the second innings, including the impressive left-hander 'Jack' Nitschke.

Thurlow, Ron Oxenham and Alec Hurwood were all good bowlers; now, with Gilbert adding an edge of pace to the attack, Queensland were genuine contenders for the Sheffield Shield. The new bowler explained his methods to the press with disarming candour. 'I do not like hitting batsmen', he said, 'I do not try to bring the ball up, but want always to go straight through, depending on my pace and straightness to get wickets. At times my deliveries get a natural swing and often, when bowling over the wicket, I swing out to leg quite a lot, but I cannot tell you when this will happen. I have not yet learned to control the swing in the air.'

§

Gilbert's emergence was timely, because Percy Hornibrook, Queensland's tall left-arm spinner, announced that he was no longer available to play any cricket outside Brisbane. Hornibrook had only just established himself in the Australian side, working his way through a powerful English batting side at the Oval to take 7-92 in the last Test of the 1930 tour. But Hornibrook was a self-employed dentist, and he could no longer afford to take several weeks away from his work each summer.

'The first-class cricket season', Arthur Mailey observed, 'is becoming more strenuous as time goes on. The New South Wales players, in common with the men of the other Sheffield States, have a busy time ahead.' Half a dozen New South Wales players were regulars in the Test side; if they played every game for their State and country in 1930-31, they would turn out in fourteen matches inside sixteen weeks, many of which involved interstate travel. As Mailey remarked, 'unless a player is a man of independent means – personally I do not know any – or interested in the sale of cricket goods – I know quite a few – or a cricket writer by profession, it will be very difficult for him to fulfil his first-class engagements.' As it happened, Alan Kippax, Bert Oldfield, Don Bradman, Archie Jackson and Stan McCabe all worked for companies selling sporting goods, who were happy to exchange time away from work for the publicity their employees attracted. But life was more difficult for players who worked in other fields. Bill Woodfull, a schoolmaster, had the benefit of the long summer vacation; others, like Alan Fairfax, found it hard to get any sort of work, and relied heavily on the £30 that the Australian Board of Control paid its players for each Test match.

§

The Melbourne Cup, Australia's best-known horse race, is run each year on the first Tuesday in November. It's usually the bookmakers' best day of the year, but in 1930 several bookies were facing certain ruin. Phar Lap was the

Herman Griffith in the Sydney nets.

Errol Hunte.

shortest-priced favourite in the history of the race, and even at the unattractive odds available, it seemed inevitable that the bookies would be obliged to make some hefty payouts.

Unless Phar Lap didn't race.

Phar Lap's strapper was Tommy Woodcock, who was intensely dedicated to the horse he nicknamed 'Bobby'. A week before the Melbourne Cup, Woodcock was approached at Harry Telford's stables by a friend of Telford's, a man 'who stood high in my estimation up to then', who calmly offered him £4,000 to dope Phar Lap the night before the big race, to ensure that he couldn't win. The mysterious intermediary, whom Woodcock never named, told the strapper that 'the Ring would never get over the knock it would receive', if Phar Lap won, and 'that he knew men who would give a heap of money to be relieved of their responsibilities'. Woodcock ordered the man off the premises, and immediately told Telford what had happened. Telford replied that more than one person would be happy if Phar Lap didn't race, and said that he'd been offered £10,000 to scratch the horse from the Cup.

Then came the letters. 'Not a day passed', Tommy Woodcock recalled, 'without my receiving a threatening letter. Phar Lap was to be sprayed with acid and poisoned needles were to be stuck into him! Such threats seemed ridiculous but it was disturbing to know that some people allowed their thoughts to run in such hideous channels. Another letter I received worried me much more than the threats about acid and poisoned needles. The writer said that if Phar Lap was not scratched he would be shot down like a dingo.'

Three days before the Melbourne Cup, Phar Lap was due to run in the Melbourne Stakes. On the morning of the race, Tommy Woodcock took him for a light run in the paddock near his stable in the Melbourne suburb of Caulfield. Riding a grey pony, Woodcock was leading Phar Lap through the streets and back to the stable when he saw a large blue Studebaker car driving towards them. The car's numberplate, he noticed, was defaced, and the passenger held a folded newspaper in front of his face. Sensing trouble, Woodcock pushed in front of Phar Lap, placing himself and the pony between the car and the racehorse. As the car drew level with Woodcock, the passenger leaned out of the window holding a double-barrelled shotgun. At that moment, Woodcock dug his heels into the side of the pony, which jerked forward, along with Phar Lap. Either for that reason, or through sheer luck, none of the pellets found their target, and the car disappeared down Glenhuntly Road.

Tommy Woodcock never named the man who tried to bribe him, and the shooter in the Studebaker was never identified. After all, more than one person would be happy if Phar Lap didn't race.

§

Upon his return to Australia, Don Bradman was given a sharp lesson on the costs and benefits of fame. In Melbourne, he was presented with a hefty cheque, representing funds raised from public subscription to recognise his exploits in England. When he arrived home at Bowral, he was greeted by a brass band playing the popular jingle 'Our Don Bradman', and General Motors presented him with a car, the Chevrolet Bradman, one of a limited edition of six (another was raffled off to raise money for the unemployed). Voters in the Sydney suburb of Granville voted to change the name of Burnett Street to Bradman Street. In the first week of November, cinemas in Australia began to show a short 'Bradman talkie', in which the cricketer demonstrated his batting technique. He had become ubiquitously, suffocatingly famous.

A civic reception was held for Bradman at the Town Hall when he returned to Sydney. 'Bradman is the Phar Lap of cricket', announced the New South Wales Chief Secretary Mark Gosling. 'Now Mr Lang is looking for new taxation schemes and I would suggest that he might impose a tax on centuries and make Don pay a super tax on every second century.' Bradman replied that if he made a blob in his next innings, people would know to blame Mr Gosling.

But he found the constant public appearances, the incessant exposure, exhausting. When he arrived for his first day back at work at the Mick Simmons store in Sydney's George Street, the crowds were so vast that a squad of policemen was needed to keep them under control. There were dinners and receptions almost every evening, among countless promotional appearances for General Motors and Mick Simmons. For an essentially introverted man, these were draining experiences. For the rest of the summer – and, really, for the rest of his life – Bradman became the focus of relentless public adulation, which he found rewarding and burdensome in equal measure. Life had been much simpler when all he had to worry about was hitting a cricket ball.

§

Jack Lang was sworn in as Premier of New South Wales on 4 November 1930, together with the members of his new cabinet. No one paid very much attention – it was Melbourne Cup day. One enterprising bookmaker had tried to stimulate interest among Sydney's punters by offering an unusual double: the New South Wales election and the Melbourne Cup. Thomas Bavin and Phar Lap were offered at 4 to 1; Jack Lang and Phar Lap were at 16 to 1, so anyone who had backed the Labor leader was now anxious for Phar Lap to do his part.

§

The Cathay docked at Fremantle, but its most famous passenger, Nellie Melba, did not disembark. She had been confined to her cabin for some days, on orders of the ship's doctor, and was 'reported to be very indisposed.' Her illness, it was said, 'was caused by heat while passing through the Red Sea.'

§

Harry Telford stood to win two-thirds of £9,225 if Phar Lap won the Cup, and he took no chances.

Two days before Cup day, he moved Phar Lap out of his Caulfield stables, hiding him away on a farm outside Geelong. At Caulfield, a horse named Old Ming was outfitted in Phar Lap's colours, red and black, and exercised in the morning to give anyone watching from a distance the impression that Phar Lap was still there. Then, on the morning of the race, Phar Lap was driven to the Flemington racetrack under a heavy police escort. Ten uniformed police surrounded the horse as he was led into his stall. No one was foolish, or desperate, enough to make another attempt to nobble Phar Lap.

It turned out that getting Phar Lap to the track was the difficult part. Once he was on the track, the race unfolded precisely as expected. Phar Lap was given the heaviest handicap – 9 stone 12 pounds – any horse had ever carried in the Melbourne Cup, and it made no difference.

A horse named Temptation set the pace early, followed by Carradale and First Acre, while Jim Pike was content to sit in fourth place, or thereabouts, and watch the others tire themselves out. Star God and Soulton each made a bid for the lead, and still Pike sat in fourth, biding his time. Then the field entered the final straight, Pike let Phar Lap go, and in a matter of seconds, the race was decided. 'When the opportunity came,' Pike said after the race, 'I gave him his head and he won like the champion he is. He had a good run, and the result was never in doubt. Phar Lap is able to do anything you ask of him. When I gave him his head, he went away from the field, and I think that had he been called upon for an extra finishing effort, he would have been well able to respond.' As it was, Phar Lap was already easing up when he crossed the line three lengths ahead of Second Wind. Temptation meandered in towards the back of the field. Soulton's jockey, Fred Dempsey, reflected that 'at the half-mile post I thought I had a splendid chance, but just then I saw Phar Lap was going so easily, I knew he had the race won.'

There was a good case for giving Phar Lap a spell after his disrupted preparation for the Melbourne Cup. But a horse earned no money for his connections standing in a stable. In the four days after the Melbourne Cup, he raced twice more, and won each time.

§

As soon as the Cathay reached Melbourne, Dame Nellie Melba was carried from the ship on a stretcher and taken by ambulance to the Mount St Evins private hospital, all without removing her fur coat. It was reported that she was 'seriously ill'. Although it was also reported that 'her indisposition is not dangerous.' One journalist noticed that the lower part of her face was bandaged, and her doctor, Richard O'Sullivan, told the press that she had 'developed a rash' from the heat, 'which had developed into painful boils'. That was not the whole truth. Melba's face was bandaged because, after singing in London, she had travelled to Paris for an operation from which she had not yet recovered – a surgical facelift.

§

In Parliament in Canberra, the Minister for Trade, James Fenton, solemnly moved that the House congratulate Charles Kingsford Smith on his record flight from London to Australia. 'Well,' heckled one backbencher, 'what about Bradman?' 'Yeah', sniped another, 'and how about Phar Lap?'

§

The *Tamaroa* docked in Wellington harbour on the morning of Wednesday, 12 November. The West Indian cricketers grabbed their passports, hustled through the immigration controls, and raced to the Basin Reserve ground, where their match against Wellington started only a few hours after their arrival.

The West Indians spent less than three days in New Zealand, and played cricket on two of them. It was a ridiculous schedule. As soon as play ended on Thursday, the team caught an overnight train to Auckland, to join the S.S. *Ulimaroa* before it sailed for Sydney on Friday morning. But the players were anxious to fit in whatever practice they could get, and were happy to run around a cricket field after three weeks at sea.

Wellington provided decent opposition; five of its top order batsmen were New Zealand Test cricketers, including the exceptional Stewie Dempster and the distinctly handy Tom Lowry. Jack Grant enjoyed a reunion with Denis Blundell, an opening bowler who had won a Cambridge blue alongside him in the 1929 University match and had since returned home, where he practiced law in Wellington (and would, years later, become the Governor-General of New Zealand). But the first day was dominated by Constantine, who took six cheap wickets in the home side's innings of 195, and fielded with a brilliance that astonished the Wellington crowd. He captured the first wicket of the tour, removing Henry Foley, and returned later in the afternoon to get rid of the stubborn Dempster, who ground out 23 dogged runs before edging a ball to Errol Hunte behind the stumps.

Jack Grant used his bowlers in short spells, switching them around frequently. Partly he wanted to avoid overworking them; partly he wanted to give everyone an opportunity; and partly he wanted to get a better understanding of what his attack looked like on a cricket ground. Tommy Scott, Frank Martin and Herman Griffith all put in decent spells. Unfortunately, the batsmen received fewer chances to work on their game, since rain delayed the start of play on the second day, and then caused an early finish, just as Frank Martin and Lionel Birkett were building a promising partnership.

George Headley made only 17 before edging a catch to the wicket-keeper. It was the one success that the bowler, Alex Newman, ever enjoyed in representative cricket – he went wicketless in his two first-class games for Wellington later in the season. Afterwards Headley told Learie Constantine that the bowlers had the ball 'swinging about through the air more than I had imagined possible.' Constantine laughed. 'Wait until you get to England. Then you will see just how much a ball can swing.'

§

The first big match of the Australian cricket season began at the Melbourne Cricket Ground on 14 November – a four day game for the benefit of the Victorian captain, Jack Ryder. A team drawn from the Australians who had toured England played against 'The Rest', who were led by Ryder. That was something of a sore point – Ryder had wanted to make the tour to England, and had unabashedly used his position as the selector nominated by Victoria to vote for himself. He had been openly furious when the other selectors opted for Stan McCabe, and his benefit match was as much a consolation as a reward for service. Rain spoiled the game as a contest, wiping out the third day when the match was evenly balanced. But the prospect of seeing Bradman in action drew a healthy crowd of 44,434 on the second day.

Bradman went to the crease early in the afternoon, after fast bowler Harry Alexander had dismissed Archie Jackson cheaply. He wasn't at all troubled by Alexander's pace, and although the elderly spinners Don Blackie and Bert Ironmonger bowled neatly, he kept the score moving with singles. The rate of scoring accelerated when Arthur Mailey took the ball. Mailey was, at 44, younger than Blackie and Ironmonger, and he still turned out in club cricket for Balmain, but hadn't played a first-class match for almost a year (and never would again). Mailey's approach to bowling was to load the ball with as much spin as he could muster, toss it up to the batsman, and challenge him to take risks. He never cared about conceding runs – which was just as well, because he often conceded plenty – as long as he had a chance of taking wickets. Bradman welcomed Mailey into the attack by running down the pitch and cracking his first ball back over his head to the boundary. A couple of overs later, he leaned back to pull a shorter ball for another four. There were loud cheers from the crowd: this was what they'd come to see. But Mailey was happy, too: as long as Bradman attacked him, he had a chance. He tried his wrong 'un, and Bradman, advancing down the pitch, misread it and was hit on the pad. An over later, he spun a sharp leg break past Bradman's outside edge. Deciding to play more watchfully, Bradman played back to the next ball, which was slightly fuller and turned a little less, clipping the off stump.

Ryder and Bill Woodfull did their best to contrive a result on the last day of the game, Ryder's declaration setting the Australians a target of 118 in 85 minutes. Again, Alexander removed Jackson, bowling him with a delivery that skidded through low, but Bradman was in excellent touch. He raced to 29 in rapid time, then skipped down the pitch and cracked a ball from Mailey straight back at the bowler. Mailey, somehow, held onto the catch. It was the last wicket he took in first-class cricket.

After the match, Mailey was modest about his own success, and quick to emphasise that he still considered Bradman a great player. 'He has everything', the leg spinner observed, 'except height.'

§

As the West Indians boarded the *Ulimaroa* in Auckland, George Headley noticed that it was a significantly smaller vessel than the *Tamaroa.* It worried him, even before the ship struck bad weather. After two days at sea, 'which were none too pleasant, the ship began to toss very badly and passengers and crew alike became very uneasy. My room-mate and I were again ill: hardly anyone could face the dining room or do any exercises. We were informed that we had run into a storm and it lasted for two days. They were certainly two wretched days – an experience I would never like to encounter again – huge waves towered above the ship and broke over her bows and the propellor periodically came out of the water, giving the impression that we were about to sink at any minute.'

Every night, Jack Grant made a point of visiting each player's cabin before he went to bed, hoping that it would somehow help. And then he turned out his own lights, because 'even a frightened person can sleep, once he has committed his ways to his Maker.'

The storm delayed the arrival of the *Ulimaroa* by almost a day, and it docked at Sydney's Darling Harbour late on the afternoon of 18 November. As they sailed beneath the Harbour Bridge, workmen suspended high above the ship waved a greeting to the tourists. Not every aspect of the welcome was so congenial. The tourists encountered, for the first time, the White Australia Policy. This was a child of the Labor Party – the unions were anxious to protect their members against competition from migrants from Asia, who might be willing to work for lower wages – and it was enforced by one of the first laws passed by the Commonwealth of Australia, the Immigration Restriction Act of 1901. This law did not actually refer to race or colour, but it empowered the Minister for Immigration to declare any immigrant a 'prohibited immigrant', for any reason or for no reason, and deport that person. The most efficient method for restricting immigration was the infamous 'dictation test', by which a migrant could be required to pass a dictation test in any European language before entering Australia. Through these means, people of an undesirable colour could be denied entry to the country, or forced to leave it. The result was that, in 1930, almost everyone in Australia had been born, either in the country, or in the British Isles. The West Indians, whose homelands were vividly multiracial, were entering a nation that – once its indigenous people had been tucked away out of sight – was conspicuously, almost uniformly, white. There is no evidence that they were ever made aware of the fact that, long before their tour began, the Australian Board of Control had been required to undertake to the Department of Home Affairs that the black members of the team would leave the country within six months of their arrival. George Headley's recollection was that 'certain clauses had been overlooked temporarily so that we could be admitted for the purpose of playing cricket.'

Like every other visitor to Australia, each West Indian was required to complete a form identifying his race. Answering it, as Headley observed, was not entirely straightforward, because 'West Indians are a cosmopolitan race in colour, shade or tan – call it what you will – primarily caused by mixed marriage.' When the players were given their immigration forms, 'one member of our contingent, who fortunately held a fairly good position in his country, and can be bracketed among West Indians as having a light tan, thought he was being clever (or maybe wished to be thought other than West Indian) and replied "European" to the question, "Colour or race?" Those of us who observed this infringement were highly amused.'

Headley proudly filled in his own form with the word, 'African'. Some of the black players simply identified themselves as 'British' – which was perfectly true, since they were subjects of the King and travelled on British passports. This puzzled the Immigration Department officials, who couldn't grasp the concept of a black British person, and instead recorded them as 'British West Indian', a nationality that did not exist.

Ivan Barrow was one of the five West Indians (along with Grant, Birkett, Wight and de Caires) whom the Australian press identified as 'white'. No one knows how answered the race question: the immigration officials listed him as 'British'. That was close enough, but his middle name was Mordecai, and his ancestors were Sephardic Jews from Portugal, a fact which he neither concealed nor advertised. He remains, to this day, the only Jewish cricketer to play for the West Indies.

§

Jack Grant had just fallen asleep on his first night in Sydney, when the telephone rang in his hotel room. It was a young woman, inviting him to a party. Grant asked her name, but 'she went on talking so I put the receiver down.' Like Phar Lap in the Melbourne Cup, Grant had overcome Temptation.

§

After spending their first night at the Hotel Sydney, the West Indians made their way to the Sydney Cricket Ground, where the No2 ground had been set aside for their practice. They had only two days to prepare for their match against New South Wales. At the nets, they were met by three former Test players, Arthur Mailey, Charles Macartney and Charles Kelleway, who volunteered their services as net bowlers. The West Indians greatly appreciated the help, although it wasn't entirely an altruistic gesture: Mailey, Macartney and Kelleway all wrote newspaper columns, and the practice sessions gave them an early opportunity to get to know the tourists.

The first net session would have been a great success, but for the fact that while the players were on the field, a thief slipped into the dressing rooms and ransacked the West Indians' wallets. Ivan Barrow lost £14, Errol Hunte £2, Lionel Birkett £1, Edwin St Hill £3/10 and Frank de Caires £3/10. The Police were called, but their investigations led nowhere. One of the victims told the press, 'You get sneak thieves in every country, even our own, and we are certainly not going to judge Sydney people by that.' Ivan Barrow's dry response was, 'Well, that doesn't altogether leave me in the ditch.'

But plenty of other people were in the ditch, as Jack Grant soon discovered. 'Wherever we went', he wrote, 'we saw large numbers of men out of work, queuing up for relief. It was a sad sight. It was also sad to see large numbers of ships in the main harbours tethered side by side and lying idle. It was sad to see empty hotels, abandoned amusement parks, poorly patronised shops, and other signs of a sagging economy. A clergyman friend took me to Botany Bay to see one of the relief camps for the unemployed. I was depressed not by the conditions in the camp but by the unhappiness and loss of hope in the faces of the men and women.'

§

The West Indians did not leave their first training session empty-handed. In exchange for the team's endorsement, each member of the squad was presented with a new pair of cream flannel 'GripU Sports Trousers'. GripU, of course, was 'the trouser with the hidden Elastic Webbing Waistband', 'cut in the latest Sports Style' with a 'Neat Pleated Waist' and 'Side and Hip Pockets'. Unless you received them as a gift, a pair of GripU trousers would set your hip pocket back by 32 shillings and sixpence.

§

The Lord Mayor of Sydney, Alderman Ernest Marks, welcomed the West Indians to the city at a reception at the Town Hall, and the following day the New South Wales Cricket Association hosted the team at a dinner at the Hotel Sydney that served not only to welcome them, but also to celebrate the achievements of the State's members of the successful Australian team. In the streets outside, there were men queuing up for servings of broth, but the cricketers dined on Fried Fillet Schnapper, Fillet de veaux Neapolitaine and Roast Turkey Anglaise. The president of the Association, Alf Green, proposed a toast to the visitors, and the Chief Justice of New South Wales, Sir Philip Street (whose grand-daughter would later marry the Test batsman Jack

Fingleton), declared that cricket was 'the greatest of British summer games'. Harry Mallett responded that 'The West Indies are British in sentiment, in tradition and in sport. And they believe cricket is an aid in the development of the fellowship or empire.' There was plenty of talk about the bonds of empire, and everyone tactfully avoided mentioning the fact that those bonds were not quite strong enough to permit a black West Indian to visit Australia without promising to leave promptly. One of the journalists present, Jack Davis, thought that 'the average of the speeches by local orators was very disappointing', noticing that 'very little seemed to be known about cricket in the West Indies by those who spoke.'

§

There was hope on the faces of the West Indians when they began their first match in Australia. Jack Grant won the toss at the SCG, took first innings before a pleasingly large crowd, and watched happily as Frank Martin and Clifford Roach built a handy opening partnership. Martin was playing with a swollen, bandaged arm after suffering an adverse reaction to a vaccination injection, but it didn't appear to trouble him. The one fastish bowler in the New South Wales attack, Gordon Stewart, made no impact; the medium-pacers, Alan Fairfax and Stan McCabe, were little more than tidy; and the leg spin of Hugh Chilvers caused no alarms. The openers posted their fifty partnership after 70 minutes, and were still batting when lunch was taken twenty minutes later. After the break, however, things fell apart. Alan Fairfax, an accurate, lively operator, removed Martin, Roach and Bartlett in quick succession. George Headley, still recovering from the effect of four weeks at sea, raced to 25, driving the ball so firmly to Alan Kippax in the covers that the fieldsman asked him, 'How do you hit the ball so hard for your size?' But then Chilvers lured him out of his crease, and Bert Oldfield made no mistake with the stumping.

Grant, Birkett and Constantine all made decent starts, on which they were unable to build. Chilvers and Stan McCabe made short work of the tail. Six of the first seven batsmen had made 18 or more, but none reached fifty, and in less than four hours the West Indians were dismissed for 188. It was a bitterly disappointing total, yet the West Indies managed to hold their hosts to a first innings lead of only 18 runs. Constantine bowled with genuine hostility, bowling Alan Fairfax late on the first evening, and then removing three Test batsmen – Kippax, Jackson and McCabe – in quick succession on the next day. One journalist reported that Constantine's fastest delivery 'has more speed than that of Larwood, and is well disguised. In fact, that ball is faster than any we have seen in the last ten years.' Arthur Mailey thought that 'New South Wales batsmen are not quite used to the pace which Constantine is capable of.' George Francis, on the other hand, deceived Bradman with a slower ball. Bradman had moved rapidly to 73, and appeared set for yet another century, when Francis gave him a ball just outside off stump, slightly short of a length. Bradman shaped up to guide the ball to third man, then tried to adjust his shot when we realised that the ball was slower than expected, and edged it through to Barrow. The third fast bowler, Herman Griffith, was left out of the side – and Francis would be omitted from the next game in Melbourne – as part of a deliberate strategy from preventing Australia's leading batsmen from seeing too much of the pace trio before the first Test.

The West Indies looked to be firmly in control of the game when Headley and Grant were compiling a fourth-wicket stand of 99 in the second innings. Headley played with greater caution this time, occasionally unfurling a fierce cut or a sweet drive; Grant was content to provide gritty support. If Headley had batted for another hour or so, his team might have been in an impregnable position, but he cracked a short ball from Chilvers just above the turf towards point, where Bradman held a sharp catch. Two balls later, Bartlett tapped the ball into the covers and ran, only to see his captain run out at the striker's end. Not long afterwards, left-armer Bill Hunt removed Bartlett, which appeared to place New South Wales back on top – except that Learie Constantine picked that moment to demonstrate his ability to turn a game on its head. In just over half an hour, Constantine belted 59 runs, alternating between deft placement and furious slogging (and winning sixpence from Charles Macartney, after betting that he would score a half century). Three times he launched Chilvers' leg-breaks onto the Hill; at the other end, he deposited a ball from Bill Hunt onto the lawn in front of the Grandstand. He was possibly unlucky that Chilvers was able to hold onto a powerful drive lashed back at the bowler. As he later recalled, 'I put every ounce of my strength behind a straight drive intended to make a hole in the bowling screen. There was no more astounded person than myself when I saw the bowler's outstretched left hand. I knew he could not hold it, but he somehow juggled his right hand to it and caught it. I saw that ball with my own eyes rebound more than a foot from the hand it first struck.' Still, he had given his team a chance: New South Wales was set a tricky target of 223.

Archie Jackson needed runs. He wasn't feeling the best, and he had failed in all his three innings since returning from England. He made a bright start, picking Constantine's slower ball and swinging it away for four, and that lifted his confidence. There were glimpses of the old Jackson; neat cuts, elegant drives, crisp strokes off his pads, even a few defiant hooks when the bowlers dropped short. With the match slipping away from him, Jack Grant gave the ball to Frank Martin, and his spinner of last resort did the trick: Wendell Bill missed a straight ball, which trapped him in front, and then Jackson, on 62, hit over a yorker. Bradman, who had moved confidently to 23, cracked Martin high over mid-off, but Headley sprinted in from the outfield and, running at full pelt, grasped a knee-high catch. When Constantine removed Bert Oldfield, New South Wales, five wickets down, still needed 92 runs. The momentum was with the West Indies, but they were frustrated by Alan Fairfax, who appealed against the light after each delivery was bowled. His persistence wore the umpires down, and finally they relented. It was a lost opportunity for the West Indies, and in more congenial conditions on the final morning, Fairfax and Stan McCabe steered their team to a four-wicket victory.

Even so, the visitors hadn't been disgraced. Despite their desperately inadequate preparation, they had pressed a powerful New South Wales team all the way. Their bowlers had adapted well to the Australian custom of eight-ball overs (although six-ball overs were to be used in the Tests). George Headley was clearly a very fine batsman, and Constantine lived up to his reputation as a vividly impactful all-rounder. Surely, when the players adjusted to their new surroundings, things could only get better.

§

The New South Wales match was also an encouraging start for the tour treasurer, Joe Scheult. On the first day, 17,830 people attended the game, and there were 28,809 on the second – the largest crowd any of the West Indians had played before. The takings at the gate amounted to £3,488, half of which Scheult claimed for the West Indies. Six more gates like that, and the tour would be in profit.

§

Hugh Chilvers, the good-natured New South Wales leg-spinner, collected nine wickets from his first meeting with the West Indian batsmen. This was a highlight of his lengthy, hopelessly unlucky career. Chilvers was almost 28 when he first played for the State, having been kept out of the side by the skills of Arthur Mailey. For a couple of seasons, he enjoyed being the leading slow bowler for New South Wales, but his pathway to the Test team was blocked by Clarrie Grimmett, and then he was eclipsed in the State side when Bill O'Reilly emerged. In only 34 first-class matches Chilvers took 151 wickets at an average of just 26, and he was obviously a Test-class bowler. But Mailey, O'Reilly and Grimmett were three of the greatest leg spinners Australia ever produced, so too often his cricket was confined to the suburban ovals of Sydney. There, he kept on playing for the Northern District club until he was fifty, taking 1153 First Grade wickets, which set a record for the competition that will never be surpassed.

§

Don Bradman announced that he would not travel to Brisbane for the Sheffield Shield match against Queensland. He was exhausted, not from playing cricket, but from his endless promotional appearances.

§

The West Indies were new to Australia, and new to Test cricket, and there hadn't been time for the Australian press to devise a nickname for the team. For a while, the influential magazine, the *Bulletin*, tried calling them 'The Buccaneers'. It didn't catch on.

§

Arthur Mailey told Learie Constantine that the crowd had enjoyed his big hitting at the Sydney Cricket Ground, especially the shot that landed in the shilling stand, a feat that hadn't been performed for years. Constantine raised an eyebrow. 'Oh, that one? Was that regarded as being a good hit? Well, if I get the chance next time, I will try to hit the ball real hard.'

§

No first-class cricket was played in Australia on Sundays. Instead, Jack Grant wrote, 'it was the wont of our assistant manager, Joe Scheult, to gather together the Roman Catholic members of our team and go off with them to mass before breakfast. On the other hand, it was my wont to gather together the non-Roman Catholic members and accompany them to matins at the nearest Anglican church.'

Ivan Barrow, presumably, slept in on Sundays.

§

In the match against Victoria in Melbourne, George Headley hit a dazzling century. Learie Constantine took 5-64. And the West Indians were massacred.

The game emphasised several of the West Indians' problems. They were too heavily reliant on their two stars. With only three games before the first Test, Grant was struggling to balance the need to get his best men into form, with the obligation to give every tourist a chance to perform. And, perhaps most important, the West Indians were not going to get the fast, bouncy pitches for which their team had been constructed. The pitch they had played on in Sydney was slower than expected, but was recognisably a cricket pitch. Yet the strip in Melbourne was something else – a big, sluggish, lifeless pudding that frustrated stroke-players and sapped the energy of the quick bowlers. George Headley remembered that 'we truly believed that we would have had fast wickets for our matches, hence our selection of so many fast bowlers. But we discovered that the wickets upon which we played had been doctored, rendering them harmless to our attack; in contrast they were amenable to spin bowling, of which our complement lacked a top-notcher. Further, the best of our batsmen were fast wicket players and were not capable of mastering a turning ball since they were continually used to playing on the hard, fast wickets of the West Indies which lend themselves to little turn. We had anticipated similar conditions.' Frank Martin had been chosen for the tour as a batsman who could occasionally contribute a few overs of spin. He bowled unathletically with a low arm, and didn't turn the ball all that much, but he was called upon to send down 28 overs against Victoria. By the end of the tour he had bowled more deliveries in the first-class matches than any of his team-mates.

First-class pitches in Australia had become increasingly docile since the resumption of cricket after the war. Groundsmen had come to be judged on their ability to produce slow, flat wickets. This didn't arise from any particular desire to disadvantage visiting teams, but from the forces exerted by cricket's economy. In a time before sponsorship and broadcasting rights, cricket lived on whatever money people paid at the turnstiles, so no groundsman was thanked for creating

Frank de Caires in Wellington.

Archie Jackson.

a pitch that produced an exciting result within two and a half days. Besides, the public enjoyed watching men like Bradman and Ponsford piling up big scores. During the 1920s, Bradman and Ponsford scored three quadruple centuries between them, and the Victorian team twice ran up totals exceeding one thousand. As long as people kept paying to watch this, there was no demand for greener, livelier pitches.

In Melbourne, the West Indians were undone by Bert Ironmonger, the 48 year old left arm spinner, who had developed his own unique method of bowling on the MCG. Ironmonger, despite the loss of the top part of his spinning finger in a childhood farmyard accident, was able to turn the ball sharply at close to medium pace. He was an austere cricketer for an austere time. He worked for the St Kilda local council, maintaining the parks and gardens, and caught the tram along St Kilda Road whenever he had a game at the Melbourne Cricket Ground. He used an ancient bat that seldom made meaningful contact with the ball, and in the field he could generally be relied upon to stop (sometimes with his feet) a ball hit directly to him, though little else. His bowling was based upon distinctly unglamorous virtues: thrift, hard work, patience, endurance. But he kept an immaculate length and wrenched spin from even the most unresponsive of pitches – sometimes with an action that, his detractors grumbled, did not entirely comply with the Laws of the game.

Ironmonger collected five wickets in the first West Indian innings, then routed the tourists with 8-31 in the second. The West Indians had never encountered a bowler like him; Headley reflected that he was faster through the air than Wilfred Rhodes, yet turned the ball more viciously. Headley, though, seldom seemed troubled by Ironmonger or anyone else. Using his feet skilfully, he drove Ironmonger straight and through cover, and handed out some harsh treatment to Victoria's new leg-spinner, Dick Hassett. Few batsmen scored freely from Ironmonger in Melbourne, but Headley peeled 55 runs from one spell of seven overs from the spinner. He reached his century in only 113 minutes.

It was a grim match for Frank de Caires and Oscar Wight. Both men needed to do well to stake a claim for a Test place, and they both failed miserably. Anchored to the crease, de Caires lasted only three balls in the first innings, surviving Bert Ironmonger's first appeal for lbw, but not the second. His second effort was even less successful, since he was lbw to Ironmonger from the second ball he faced. Two innings, five balls, three appeals, no runs. It was a cruel initiation. Wight, a specialist batsman, resented being sent in to bat at eight and nine in the order; he clouted a boundary in each innings, and was twice out for seven.

The night before Victoria batted, the West Indians had gone to the cinema, where they saw a short celebrating the performance of the Australian cricketers in England and praising the captain, the 'unbowlable' Bill Woodfull. 'No! I'll bowl him tomorrow!' Constantine announced, and he did, before Woodfull had scored a run. It made little difference. In between the two West Indian collapses, Victoria ran up 594 runs in only 446 minutes. Ponsford serenely accumulated 187; the more aggressive Keith Rigg pressed his claims for Australian selection with a vigorous 126. It was possible to score runs on these pitches; the West Indians just hadn't yet learned how.

§

As the West Indians struggled against Victoria, many citizens of Melbourne avoided the cricket and went instead to a competing entertainment – the trial for murder of Richard Buckley. The prosecution case relied heavily on evidence of the victim's identification of Buckley (from police photographs) before his death – something the law knows as a dying declaration. There could be no testimony from Buckley's accomplice Murray, who'd been hanged, or from Squizzy Taylor, who'd died in a shooting in 1927. But the police managed to assemble several witnesses who had been at Glenferrie Station on the day of the murder.

They were cross-examined by Buckley's counsel, George Arnot Maxwell KC. Maxwell was regarded as the leading criminal silk at the Melbourne bar even though, in 1929, he had become totally blind. He was usually led into the courtroom by his wife, who dressed in solemn black for murder trials. When not in court, Maxwell was often in Parliament, sitting in the Victorian House of Representatives as a Nationalist member (although he voted almost as often with Labor). He was a devout Presbyterian, Scottish-born – although his maternal grandmother had been a black Jamaican woman. Maxwell's usual approach to a case was to begin by convincing himself of his client's innocence, before urging the jury to join him in that belief. But he lacked the ruthlessness of the best cross-examiners.

A stronger cross-examiner might have demolished the evidence identifying Buckley as the murderer. None of it was especially compelling, although the witnesses did their best to recall an event that they had glimpsed only fleetingly, seven years ago. 'He has the build of the man I saw at Glenferrie', said one witness, 'but I can't swear to his features.' 'He is not so gross in the body as the man I saw', was the evidence of another. Norman Rattray, who had identified Angus Murray, 'did not see the short man'. William James did see the short man, but thought that he 'looked about forty', which was only out by twenty years. Charles Huggins testified that he had identified Buckley from a photograph in 1923, but when he was shown two old photographs of Buckley, said that neither of them was the one he had seen. Henry Farey admitted that 'It is hard for me to recognise the man now. The man I saw was clean shaven.' What about his features? 'I would not like to say.'

It took the jury five minutes to find Buckley guilty.

§

In the middle of Buckley's trial, Sydney's *Sunday Pictorial* devoted an entire page to a short story by the West Indian wicket-keeper, Errol Hunte – The Soul's Awakening. It would be pointlessly cruel to critique the style of the piece, beyond observing that it's probably as accomplished a work of short fiction as any ever published by a Test match wicket-keeper. And, anyway, the story is propelled by narrative rather than style. It's a little morality tale, heavy on exposition and allegory. Late on Christmas Eve, Richard Seymour leaves his apartment intending to kill his best friend, George Fairwright. Richard, recently released from prison, blames George for everything that has gone wrong with his life – it was George who married the girl Richard loved, and George who reported Richard's embezzlement to their employer. On his way to meet George, Richard encounters two acquaintances, Mr Noble and Mr Malice. They're unlikely companions: 'Malice was sallow-complexioned, with a hawk-nose and evil-looking eyes', while 'Noble's countenance was pleasant and open as a baby's.' Noble tries to persuade Richard not to go through with the murder; Malice encourages his dark instincts. Readers familiar with tales of this kind might expect Noble's arguments to prevail but, curiously, what eventually sways Richard from his grim purpose isn't a moral epiphany or Noble's appeal to his better nature, but his own fear of 'the final walk escorted by two warders and the prison officials. The dull tramp of feet. The hangman's expressionless face... the gallows!'

The twist is, Richard then wakes up. It was a dream – although how much of it was a dream, we're not told. Maybe Richard was an embezzler, fresh out of jail – it isn't clear, but it doesn't matter, because the church bells are ringing, 'peace on earth, goodwill to men', and everything is going to be all right.

§

King George V was unhappy. He had granted an audience, in London, to the visiting Prime Minister Scullin, at which Scullin sought royal approval for the appointment of a new Governor-General. Scullin's nominee was Sir Isaac Isaacs, the Chief Justice of the High Court of Australia, a man of formidable and forthright intellect. There had been eight governors-general appointed in the thirty years since Australian federation: all of them had been British, several had been minor aristocrats and most had been Conservative politicians. Lord Stonehaven, whose term ended on 2 October 1930, had been both. Sometimes the appointment was made as a reward for service, and sometimes it was a useful means of removing an irritating factional opponent from London. Scullin believed, as a matter of principle, that the King's representative in Australia ought to be Australian, but there was also the money to consider. Appointing the famously frugal Isaacs (who subsisted largely on vast quantities of cold tea) would be a significantly cheaper exercise than transporting, housing and maintaining an Earl or a Baron. Scullin took advantage of the fact that, while there was no clear protocol on how the appointment of the governor-general was to occur, the King was required to act on the advice of his ministers. Despite suggestions that the King should be provided with options, he presented George V with a single nomination, Isaacs. 'Received Mr Scullin', the King grumbled in his diary, 'and he told me he wished to appoint Sir Isaac Isaacs as the new Governor-General of Australia. He argued with me for some time — and with great reluctance I had to approve of the appointment. I should think it would be very unpopular in Australia.' It was widely believed (but cannot be proved) that the King was unwilling to appoint Isaacs partly because, besides not being English, he was Jewish. As it happened, the appointment was almost universally well-received – except by John Latham, the Leader of the Opposition in the Australian Parliament, who protested that the King should have made the appointment 'on the advice of British Ministers' and that now 'the reality of the bond of Empire will be diminished.'

§

'When we went to Australia', Learie Constantine reflected, 'I felt just a shade uneasy, in common with others in the side, of the sort of reception black players might receive in a country where the colour bar causes high feelings.' It was a sensible concern: urban Australians, with the purity of their nation cocooned by the White Australia Policy and most of their own indigenous people consigned to remote settlements, hardly ever encountered a black man.

The West Indians could not hope to avoid racism in Australia; on the contrary, they faced it every day. It was commonplace for newspaper reports of their matches to identify players by the colour of their skin – 'Grant (white)', or 'Headley (coloured)' – and a great deal of ink was spilled to inform readers whether players were 'chocolate brown' or 'ebony-hued'. The newspaper caricatures of the black players invariably resorted to atrocious racist tropes – big lips, huge teeth, frizzy hair, grotesquely elongated limbs. The players were routinely referred to as 'the dusky visitors', or in Constantine's case, 'the dusky freak', because his fielding was 'as active as a monkey'. One Queensland newspaper reported a West Indian batting collapse under the headline, 'A Black Out'.

And yet what the West Indians experienced was not hostility, so much as ignorance and amiable stupidity. Most of the West Indian cricketers belonged to the black middle class, a notion that was incomprehensibly alien to Australia. Australians who had never met black people formed their expectations of them – as primitives – from a culture saturated with the crudely parodic stereotypes perpetuated in books and films. Tarzan movies, full of fierce jungle savages, were especially popular, and the most successful film of 1930 was the Ziegfeld musical *Whoopee!*, an early Technicolor talkie in which Eddie Cantor spends much of his time cavorting ludicrously in blackface. Accustomed to seeing black people portrayed as angry cannibals or comic stooges, many Australians were unprepared for the fact that most of the West Indian players had received more education, and held more demanding jobs, than their Australian counterparts. The Bishop of Toowoomba expressed great surprise on discovering that 'the West Indies cricketers, although mostly black in colour, are highly cultured.'

Not everyone received the message. Lionel Birkett recalled a reception at which 'a host asked one of our team of African descent to say a few words in his native language. We all spoke only English, but St Hill immediately brought forth a most amazing flow of sounds which he then translated as "We have been very delighted in the very friendly way in which we have been treated by both your public and your cricketers and thank you all."' Something similar happened at Newcastle, where the local dignitary sitting next to Herman Griffith jabbed a finger in Constantine's direction, and grinned, 'Him! Great! Bat!' Griffith sighed, gave a weary smile, and responded, 'Yes. You know, I firmly believe that his prowess is hereditary. His father was an excellent cricketer and has trained him in the intricacies of the game, but many of his strokes come to him instinctively.' The Labor Daily cautioned its readers against making mistakes of this kind, warning them that 'the coloured players speak with a pleasing English accent, and some of their rejoinders could be expected from Oxford men'.

At the end of the tour, Constantine concluded that 'there was never the slightest hint of any discrimination against us, either by onlookers or players or officials. We were just treated as cricketers, given a magnificent time, and made to feel friendliness wherever we went.' Some of this might have been true. There's a persistent story, of the kind that through repeated telling solidifies into a received truth, that when the West Indians first arrived in Sydney, their hosts had booked separate hotels for the white and coloured players. But there's absolutely no evidence that this ever occurred. One unintended consequence of the White Australia Policy was that, within the country itself (and with the important and shameful exception of the treatment of indigenous people), there was little institutionalised segregation – there was no call for it, since the immigration system had excluded coloured people already. But it's also true that much of the 'friendly' treatment the West Indians received would not be tolerated today. In Adelaide, for example, it was reported that the tourists 'were barracked good-humouredly in the mixture of Americanisms and baby talk, in which one might address a crude negro vaudeville artist.'

The West Indies team itself wasn't entirely free from racial tensions. As Grant put it, 'at home there is a saying that we play together, worship together, do business together, but do not mix much socially.' The fact that the team's leaders were all white – manager, assistant manager, captain and vice-captain – was an uncomfortable reflection of the social distinctions that still prevailed in the West Indies. Early in the tour, Grant admitted, 'on one occasion when things were not going well, I "ticked off" a player in anger; and I did so, inadvisedly, in front of others. He replied in language that savoured of "White man, stop talking to me as a black boy." It was as upsetting as it was helpful. That night I hardly slept. Before breakfast the following morning, I knocked at the door of the player concerned. Having entered his room, I said to him, 'I'm sorry for our clash yesterday.' This helped to clear the air, and we were able to talk to each other in a much more mature way. From then on, we were on much better terms, and never again did we have such a clash.'

§

At one dinner attended by the West Indian team, Edwin St Hill found himself seated beside a curious Australian who wanted to know 'what you usually eat in the West Indies?' He was tempted to answer, 'leaves and stones', before he restrained himself.

Increasingly, what Australians usually ate – especially in Queensland and New South Wales – was choko. Choko – sechium edule – is an edible gourd distantly related to pumpkin and squash, native to North America but introduced to Australia some time in the late nineteenth century. The fruit, which has an unappealing, thick, crinkled green skin, is roughly the size and shape of a pear, and grows

grows – easily and abundantly – on vines. During the Depression, choko vines were slung over backyard fences all over the country to provide a cheap source of food. Choko grew all year round, was filling, and was a reasonably good source of vitamin C. It just didn't taste of anything much at all.

In good times, no-one willingly ate choko if anything better was available. But in the Depression its very blandness became an asset. Salt it, and the choko was your vegetable – add some sugar, and it was your fruit. Newspapers and magazines published hundreds of choko recipes: there was choko pie (add sugar and lime juice, slice thinly, bake) and choko jam (livened up by a dash of ginger). If boiled choko were served as a vegetable, it was recommended that it be accompanied by a thick onion sauce. Choko pickles could be prepared in salt water, together with cabbage or cauliflower. If you were feeling particularly adventurous – or if you were really, really sick of choko – you could even hide it in a curry.

It was harder to find something to accompany the choko. Even though meat was impossibly expensive, shortages were frequent. The spectacularly alcoholic Sydney journalist, Lennie Lower, found it curious that even though 'there may be a meat shortage… we can always get sausages!' Things, Lower observed, 'are not as they used to be. Once the wife could go into the shop and, after poking her finger into every bit of meat about the place, demand the first cut of the rump. Now she sneaks in the back entrance on her hands and knees and whines, "Have you got any meat?" The butcher laughs hoarsely all over his apron, and chopping a piece of bloodstained wood off his chopping block, says, "Madam, I was keeping this for myself, but as you're a good customer…"'

So for protein, usually, there was rabbit. One occupation flourished above all others during the Depression – the 'rabbitoh'. The rabbitoh trapped or caught rabbits – or knew someone who did – killed them, and went from door to door selling them. The job took its name from the vendors' distinctive call of 'rabbit – oh!' each time they entered a new street. Rabbit sold cheaply, so the rabbitoh's returns were meagre, but his costs were vanishingly small, so he generally finished up ahead. There was even a celebrity rabbitoh – Stephen Gascoigne, better known as 'Yabba', who was known for his noisy, caustic barracking from the Hill at the Sydney Cricket Ground. If you could find and afford beef or chicken, lamb or pork, you'd ignore the rabbitoh; but in the crowded inner city areas of Sydney, Melbourne and Brisbane, most people couldn't.

An entire generation of Australians grew up during the Depression, silently vowing never again to eat choko or rabbit.

§

Queensland remained, improbably, at the top of the Sheffield Shield table, after taking first innings points from a batting duel with New South Wales. Alan Kippax, Stan McCabe and Wendell Bill all hit centuries for New South Wales in a massive first innings of 566, which might have been even larger had Eddie Gilbert (who took four wickets) not bowled so well. After conceding similar totals in the previous season, Queensland had usually surrendered meekly, but this time they stunned the visitors by responding with a colossal 687. Frank Gough, the captain, hit 137 and the forty-year old veteran, Cecil Thompson, batted for ten and a half hours to amass 275 not out. All sorts of records tumbled – the total was the highest Queensland had ever recorded (and remained so until 2006), while Thompson's marathon innings was not only the first double-century for the State in the Sheffield Shield, but would remain the highest individual score for Queensland for more than thirty years. More importantly, Queensland looked to have assembled a team capable of mounting a realistic challenge for the title.

Yet possibly Archie Jackson enjoyed the game more than anyone. Sunday, the last day of November, was a rest day, and Frank Gough invited the New South Wales team to join him at a tennis party. There, Gough introduced Jackson to Phyllis Thomas. She was 19, a little younger than Jackson, and had trained as a ballet dancer. But in Brisbane during the Depression, there was little demand for performances of *Swan Lake*; instead, Phyllis found work as a member of the Exquisite Eight, a popular music hall troupe who 'gave excellent exhibitions and gracefully executed steps' but would also 'gracefully parade in bathing dress' and occasionally 'left the audience dumbfounded by their bodily contortions'. Jackson was smitten. It may be no coincidence that, in the second New South Wales innings, he showed his best form of the season so far, cracking 53 sparkling runs.

§

'I really think the Australians are a wonderful lot of people', Tommy Scott told the *Kingston Gleaner*. 'They are all "bonza" chaps, to use their own expression. A "bonza" chap in Australia is what we would call out in Jamaica, a jolly good fellow.'

On this point, opinions differed. When Sir Otto Niemeyer left Australia in late November, he reported to the governor of the Bank of England, Montagu Norman, that the Australian government was 'leaderless and stupid' and that Australians were 'utterly ignorant of economics'. Their politicians understood about one quarter of what he said, and there was 'an extraordinary absence of constructive criticism. The personnel all round – political, administrative and banking – is, with rare exceptions, lamentable.' Australia, he concluded, was overpopulated. Further settlement there should be discouraged.

Tommy Scott.

5

December

Australia wins the first Test; Richard Buckley gets a reprieve; Don Bradman gets a fine; Learie Constantine gets a hundred; and Oscar Wight misses the boat.

As soon as their match against Victoria ended, the West Indians boarded the train for Adelaide, where they had a game against South Australia before the first match of the Test series. Already it was clear that their batsmen were vulnerable to good spin bowling, and a visit to Adelaide meant playing against Clarrie Grimmett on his home turf.

A short, spindly, bald man, Grimmett was an unlikely-looking menace. But he was, like Phar Lap, a transplanted New Zealander at the peak of his powers. He had arrived in Australia as an ambitious but ordinary trundler from Wellington, and through sheer determination and hard work, had turned himself into the best leg-spinner in international cricket. In Sydney, he bowled well in club cricket without earning a place in the State side; in Victoria, he played a handful of first-class matches without establishing himself. He needed to move to South Australia to play regularly in first-class cricket, and he was 33 when he played his first Test match. He marked his debut by taking 6-37 and 5-45 against England, and he had been an automatic selection for Australia ever since. He carried the Australian attack in England in 1930, taking 29 wickets in the Test series – no other bowler on either side managed more than 15. 'We could have played any team without Don Bradman', Vic Richardson explained when he arrived home, 'but we would not have beaten the blind school without Grimmett.' Partly, of course, this was a shot at Bradman, whom Richardson disliked, but it was an accurate assessment of Grimmett's importance to the team.

Grimmett bowled with an unusually low arm and, as leg spinners go, he wasn't an extravagant spinner of the ball. But he had immaculate control, enough turn to beat the bat, and plenty of variety. No bowler ever spent more time thinking about the game than Grimmett, who had a theory for every occasion, and a plan for every batsman.

None of this intimidated Clifford Roach. In the State game, the

West Indians batted first, and Roach and Birkett started briskly against the medium pace of Tim Wall and Tom Carlton. Grimmett was entrusted with the ninth over of the innings, and Roach immediately ran down the pitch and launched a mighty drive over the long boundary at mid-on. Roy Lonergan, fielding in the deep, made a desperate effort to intercept the ball, but ended up colliding with the fence and knocking himself unconscious. Birkett was out not long afterwards, caught in the deep from Philip Lee's off spin, but Roach and George Headley continued to attack Grimmett, advancing down the pitch at every opportunity. After only 80 minutes, the score passed 100, with only one wicket down.

It was too good to last. Roach was caught on the fence in the last over before lunch; then, after Headley was run out, Grimmett demolished the middle order. The last nine wickets fell for only 68 runs. Grimmett emerged from the innings with four wickets and plenty of ideas about how he'd bowl in the Test match.

The West Indies fought back, reducing South Australia to 53 for four after some fine bowling by George Francis and brilliant fielding by Roach and Constantine, each of whom executed a run out. But, with Tommy Scott resting, they had no front-line spinner in the side, and when the ball softened, South Australia's lower order scored at will. Clarrie Grimmett hit fifty; worse still, Charlie Walker and Tim Wall added 93 for the last wicket, with Wall scoring the only half-century he ever made in his 108 first-class matches. The West Indian second innings was almost a copy of the first; after the openers added fifty, the innings collapsed to Grimmett, who collected five more wickets. South Australia won by ten wickets.

§

On the morning of Sunday, 7 December, Dr Nutter Thomas, the Bishop of Adelaide, heard movement in the nave of St Peter's Cathedral, half an hour before his morning service was due to begin. When he went out to see what was happening, he found Jack Grant and half a dozen West Indian cricketers, sitting quietly

Richard Buckley.

Oscar White.

in pews and waiting for the service to start. They had been misinformed about the time of the service. In his sermon, Thomas remarked that he had never seen so many cricketers at a service, and had never seen anyone wait so patiently for one.

§

Jack Grant began the tour acutely aware that he had no meaningful experience of captaincy, and was wise enough to know that he needed advice. Lionel Birkett was his designated vice-captain, but Birkett had even less experience than Grant. And so, in the first few matches of the tour, Grant took to consulting Learie Constantine on bowling changes and field placings.

This didn't please everyone. Oscar Wight played only once in the first four matches, had no realistic chance of playing himself into the Test team, and was angry about it. He attributed his misfortune to the fact that 'from the beginning of the tour, it was evident that a slightly wrong impression as to the capabilities of the individual players had been gained by our captain. With no experience of his men, I am inclined to think that he paid too much attention to advice which was prejudiced by a feeling that he little expected even existed.' Wight blamed this prejudice on 'Trinidadians', and by Trinidadians, he meant Constantine, whose influence over the captain he resented. 'I am certain', he wrote after the tour, 'that two of our best bowlers would have requested return tickets had their choice of ends or length of spells with the ball continued to rest upon the decision of another bowler.'

Grant had other things on his mind – particularly, his own batting. His first encounter with Clarrie Grimmett had been disastrous. In his first innings in Adelaide, the *Advertiser* reported, 'he faced only a few balls from Grimmett and knew nothing about any of them.' He hadn't scored when he tapped a tame catch to silly mid-on. In the second innings, he tried to attack, but had scored only one when he skied an easy return catch to Grimmett. He had only three more days in which to work out a method for surviving against the leg-spinner.

§

The Australian government spent a great deal of time over the summer wrestling with the problem of sugar. A substantial sugar industry, centred on the state of Queensland, had developed in the late years of the nineteenth century. Cultivating and harvesting sugar was labour-intensive, and to keep costs down, the canefields were manned by workers imported – often against their will – from the Pacific islands. After Australia's federation, the importation of islander workers offended the White Australia Policy, so a Federal law was passed in 1904, putting an end to the practice. White workers, however, insisted on higher wages and better working conditions, and those demands threatened the profitability of the industry. So, to prevent Australia from being flooded with cheaper imports of what was known bluntly as 'black-grown sugar' from the West Indies, prohibitive tariffs were introduced, followed ten years later by an embargo on imports. By 1930, the value of the embargo was being challenged by free trade advocates, who argued that consumers were disadvantaged by their inability to buy less expensive sugar from the West Indies, and a Federal Sugar Inquiry was established to investigate the industry. Its commissioners spent the summer travelling through the country, hearing evidence from witnesses in every State.

The Inquiry eventually reached the conclusion that cheap sugar could be produced only if it were grown by black men working for low wages. That left Australia with a choice between protecting its sugar industry from competition, or allowing the sugar growers to use black labour. *The Land*, Australia's rural newspaper, warned that if black labour were reintroduced, then 'tropical Australia, lacking its present stalwart garrison of white defenders, would be helpless to resist invasion. In short, our cherished White Australia policy, destituted of validity, would be flung to the wolves of chance.'

The Inquiry, to no-one's surprise, recommended that the embargo on imports should remain in place.

§

Australia's team for the first Test contained six players from New South Wales, who caught a train from Sydney to Melbourne, where they connected with the train to Adelaide. Before boarding the train, they were met by Charles Bull, the treasurer of the Australian Board of Control, who handed them each a cheque for £150. Except for Bradman.

The Australians who toured England in 1930 were each paid £600, in several instalments – one of £50 before the tour began, £80 each month during the course of the tour, and a final payment of £150 after the tour had ended and the manager had submitted his report to the Board. This last instalment was generally known as 'good conduct money', since it could be withheld if the manager's report showed that a player had misbehaved on the tour. The Board made no announcement about this, but the news leaked almost immediately. There was feverish speculation about what Bradman might have done to merit the withholding of his good conduct money. Journalists asked Bradman himself for comment. But he still wasn't talking to the press.

§

There's no clear record of how the West Indian cricketers were compensated for their tour. An early report suggested that the West Indies Board intended to pay each player an outfitting allowance of £50 before the tour began, and expenses of £2 a week during the tour. It's likely that the final arrangements were similar to that. Possibly there were separate negotiations with the two professionals, Constantine and Francis, and one report suggested that they were each paid £250, but no one would have finished the tour very much wealthier than he had been at the start.

It was quite possible, however, for a player to go through the tour without having to pay for his own food or entertainment. Wherever they went in Australia, the West Indians were deluged with invitations to dinners, receptions and opportunities to view the local sights. In Adelaide, Learie Constantine was invited to play a round of golf, an invitation he declined politely, pointing out that 'we get quite enough exercise chasing cricket balls that the other fellow knocks about the field without chasing a ball one hits oneself.' The Mayor of Glenelg invited them to visit the beachside suburb, including the beach and Luna Park. But Tommy Scott had different priorities. He wanted to visit prisons.

Scott was the chief warder of the St Catherine's District Prison in Jamaica. The government of Jamaica, he reasoned, had been kind enough to grant him leave to make the tour, so it was his duty to visit as many penal institutions as he could in Australia, to see whether he could learn anything that would help him in his work. He visited two prisons in Sydney, Pentridge in Melbourne, and Yatala in Adelaide, as well as meeting with prison officials in each city. At Pentridge, he was shown the maximum security cells, where Richard Buckley was awaiting execution.

Tommy Scott spent the whole of his working life in the Jamaican prisons system. In 1944, he established a new prison, the Richmond Farm Correctional Centre, a low-security jail for first offenders, who were put to work on a banana plantation. The prison, Scott said, was planned using ideas he had gathered while on tour in Australia. Richmond Farm is where Bunny Wailer served time after he was arrested for possession of cannabis in 1967, and it's still in service today.

Scott wasn't the only member of the West Indies team with a more serious purpose than cricket. Jack Grant was always highly conscious that 'cricket was a game, it was not my life' and 'I could not give it the priority that others did.' And Learie Constantine surprised Australian reporters when he told them, 'If I find cricket interferes with my appointed goal, then cricket must go. A man who has nothing to show after years of cricket is called a fool, and he is treated worse than a man who has done nothing. Cricket with me is a means to an end, and that end is to be a lawyer.'

§

Richard Buckley decided not to appeal against his conviction. Instead, he made a careful political calculation. It was routine for capital sentences to be referred to the State Cabinet, which had the power to commute them, but a Victorian State election was imminent – Premier Edmond Hogan was likely to call one at any time. Hogan's Labor Party might very well lose to the Nationalist Party, the difference between the two being, as far as Buckley was concerned, that the Labor Party opposed capital punishment while the Nationalists supported it with grim enthusiasm. If Buckley appealed, and lost, he ran the risk that the government might have changed in the meantime, in which case he had no prospect of his sentence being commuted. His best chance was to leave the decision on his sentence up to Hogan's Cabinet.

Buckley's strategy paid off. On Tuesday 9 December, the State Cabinet announced that his sentence would be commuted to imprisonment for life, citing Buckley's age and the time that has passed since his crime was committed. He served 15 years, and was released in 1946 when prison doctors determined that he was close to death. He lived for another seven years.

He also lived to see the downfall of his nemesis, Detective Fred Lacey, who (along with Detective Coffey) was dishonourably discharged from the police force in 1933, after he was accused of corruptly assisting Patrick Bolger, a prominent cocaine dealer. Unhappily for posterity, reports of that episode do not reveal how Lacey dressed for his meeting with Bolger.

§

Australia handed a Test debut to Alec Hurwood, a Queenslander who bowled off-breaks at brisk medium pace. Hurwood had endured an unhappy tour of England, where he appeared to play no part at all in Bill Woodfull's plans. In the twelve matches Australia played before the first Test, Hurwood was given only 99 overs, which made it plain that his captain had no intention of using him in the Ashes series. Even after the Tests began, and Hurwood could have helped to rest the frontline bowlers in county games, there were matches when he bowled no more than half a dozen overs. His length was always immaculate, and he was very economical, conceding just two runs an over throughout the course of the tour. The editor of *Wisden* remarked that 'of Hurwood curiously enough not much was seen. That a bowler able to spin the ball as he could should not have had more opportunities certainly caused a good deal of surprise. Although never scored off with any approach to freedom, he was rarely kept on for any reasonable spell.' Archie Jackson, Hurwood's room-mate for the England tour, agreed, insisting that 'at times he was out of luck, but at others was really dangerous. It appeared to me that there was no reason for Hurwood to be taken off at frequent intervals, and just when he looked like getting wickets.'

Now that Percy Hornibrook was unavailable, the Australian selectors had a place to fill. Bert Ironmonger would have been a like-for-like replacement for the left-arm spinner, but perhaps the selectors felt that Hurwood was owed a proper opportunity. Hurwood kept his thoughts to himself, and celebrated his selection by taking 7-47 for his Brisbane club, Valley.

§

Queensland wasn't accustomed to sitting at the top of the Sheffield Shield ladder. Its players and officials weren't quite sure how to behave in that position. So they decided to tear each other apart.

During the home match against New South Wales in Sydney, the Queensland Cricket Association had filmed Eddie Gilbert's bowling from various different angles. They were confident that umpires in Brisbane wouldn't call him for throwing, but couldn't feel so sure about officials in the south. After viewing the film several times in a private meeting, the selectors decided that it was safe to name Gilbert in the team to tour the southern states, and the QCA began to negotiate with the Protector of Aboriginals the terms on which Gilbert would be permitted to travel.

At that point, Queensland's captain, Frank Gough, telephoned one of the selectors and announced that he would not go on tour if Gilbert were selected. Gilbert, he said, was hard to manage in the field, besides which 'there is a social side to the tour,' and Gilbert's presence would interfere with it. He added that he had also heard that the selectors proposed to name the eleven for each game of the tour, rather than leaving the selections to the captain and senior players, as had occurred in the past. Gough's comments were not well received. He was told that if he wished to withdraw from the tour, he could do so, because Gilbert was definitely going. And he was informed that the Queensland selectors intended to pick the teams on tour because at the start of the season, Cecil Thompson had told one selector that 'it would be a cricket calamity' if Gough were chosen as captain, while Ron Oxenham had criticised Gough's captaincy to another. Ordinarily, Gough and his senior players, Thompson and Oxenham, would have formed the tour selection committee, but the selectors had no confidence that those three players could work together harmoniously.

Frank Gough grumbled, but he agreed to go on tour. Before the team caught the train to Sydney, he was given his instructions by the senior selector, James Holdsworth: Gordon Amos, a medium pacer who could bat usefully, was to be twelfth man against New South Wales. Gough protested that he needed Amos in the eleven, as cover in case Gilbert was no-balled. It was too late, he was told: the team had been chosen.

When they reached Sydney, the entire team convened a meeting. Pud Thurlow chaired it, Vic Goodwin acted as secretary, and the team voted unanimously to appoint Gough, Thompson and Oxenham as tour selectors. The three men put their differences to one side, and sat down to pick the team. Gordon Amos needed to play, they decided, and they left out Gordon

Bourne (a precocious seventeen year-old) instead. It probably made little difference to the outcome of the game; Amos took a single wicket, and didn't bat for all that long. But Queensland stunned New South Wales by taking the points for a first innings lead. Batting first, they made only 166, Vic Goodwin batting bravely for 62. That total looked hopelessly inadequate when Jack Fingleton steered New South Wales to 80 for one. But then Goodwin chipped out left-hander Alec Marks, and Eddie Gilbert triggered a startling collapse in which six wickets tumbled for 25 runs. Hugh Chilvers and Bill Hunt fought hard for a while, but Gilbert returned to wrap up the innings, and Queensland led by 23. Vic Goodwin then hit another half-century, Gilbert lashed 24 unlikely runs, and Queensland set New South Wales 393 to win. The home team might have succeeded – it reached 212 for one – had the final day not been washed out entirely. So after three matches, half its program, Queensland was unbeaten and in first place on the Shield table, with 11 points from a possible 15.

And the administrators of the Queensland Cricket Association were furious.

§

The West Indies team for the first Test almost selected itself. Among the batsmen, de Caires, Wight and Sealy had staked no sort of claim to a place in the side, and just as obviously, St Hill was the superfluous bowler. The only real choice for Jack Grant to make was whether Errol Hunte or Ivan Barrow would keep wicket. Both men had performed adequately, but no better than adequately, behind the stumps, and each had scraped together some useful runs without making a substantial score. There was no clear way to split the two players, and perhaps Grant opted for Barrow in order to prove that he was free from any Trinidad bias.

Economically, socially and politically, Australia was in chaos, but it still fielded the world's most formidable cricket team, and its opponents had lost three straight matches against state sides. There was a colossal discrepancy in experience between the two sides. Clifford Roach was the most experienced Test player on the West Indian team, having appeared in all seven of the West Indies' matches since 1928; but Bert Oldfield, who had played Test cricket since 1920, had 25 caps. Learie Constantine had played 73 first-class games, many more than any other West Indian; five of the Australians had played in more than one hundred. The West Indian captain and vice-captain would both be appearing in Test cricket for the first time.

Grant won the toss, and had no doubts about batting first on a true pitch under bright skies. Tim Wall bowled the first ball in Test cricket between Australia and the West Indies, and Clifford Roach clipped it away off his legs for two runs. Roach, always a sharp dresser, made the stroke from under the brim of a smart Panama hat. Wall's early spell was expensive; Lionel Birkett punched a boundary past cover, then hit a square cut to the fence, while Roach edged a lucky stroke through the slips for four, and then pulled a short ball high over square leg for six. At the other end, Alan Fairfax was accurate but unthreatening. The first fifty runs came after only 36 minutes of play.

Predictably, it was Clarrie Grimmett who put an end to that promising start. He deceived Birkett in the flight, and the batsman could only chip back a gentle catch to the bowler. George Headley then defended carefully for three balls, only to pat the fourth softly to Tim Wall at silly mid-on. But Roach and Frank Martin held firm until the lunch break. Martin was the only left-hander in the West Indies top order, and he played Grimmett, who turned the ball in towards his bat, more confidently than the right handers. Twice in an over, he drove the leg-spinner to the fence.

But when the West Indies lost wickets, they lost them in clusters. Roach swatted a ball from Tim Wall to the boundary to raise his fifty, but shortly afterwards, he leaned forward to a ball from Hurwood, and Bert Oldfield completed a smart stumping. Constantine decided to attack Grimmett, an exercise that lasted for only three balls. Then Grimmett turned a ball through Martin's defence, and the West Indies were in deep trouble at 131 for five. They were rescued by two contrasting performances. Jack Grant settled in doggedly, and ground out his runs through sheer determination. Against Grimmett, he relied on stubbornness and hope, and the elimination of any possible risk, so that long stretches of time passed without Grant scoring at all – in 42 minutes, either side of the tea interval, he added not a single run. That was unimportant, though, because at the other end, Edward Bartlett took control. Bartlett adopted a simple method, blocking anything that was straight, and hurling his bat at the ball whenever he was offered any width. He was a short man, able to hit hard off the back foot whenever the ball was even slightly short. He was at his best against the quicker bowlers; when the new ball was taken, he welcomed it by hammering Fairfax for three boundaries in an over, through cover, midwicket and mid-on. Before long, Grimmett took the ball again, and he removed Bartlett with a quicker ball that skidded through straight. Bartlett had scored 84 of the 114 runs he added with his captain. Grant was still there at the end of the innings, unbeaten on 53 after more than three hours of watchful defence.

One reason for Grant's success, apart from sheer grit, was that he had decided to break up Grimmett's line and length by sweeping – something which none of the other specialist batsmen attempted. It would have been interesting to see how The Broom fared against Australia's spinners, and he would at least have afforded Grant a different tactical option. But he was busy playing soccer in Jamaica, and no one else, Constantine apart, was prepared to play with Passailaigue's audacity.

Archie Jackson and Bill Ponsford provided Australia with a serene start, and by lunch on the second day they had posted a half-century partnership. After the interval, however, they were unsettled by a lively spell from George Francis. Francis adopted the simple approach of bowling at a decent pace, just outside off stump, moving the ball a little off the pitch and challenging the batsmen to take risks if they wanted to score. Jackson nicked a catch through to Ivan Barrow, and then Ponsford edged the ball to first slip, where Birkett held a good, diving catch. The big wicket, as always, was Bradman. He began confidently, clipping Constantine away for two. But when he had made only four, Herman Griffith tempted him into a loose shot outside off stump, and Grant clutched the catch in the slips. Australia was 64 for three, Bradman was gone and, just for a moment, the West Indians were on top. The first ball Alan Kippax faced, from George Francis, crashed into his pads and the West Indians roared an appeal. Umpire George Hele slowly shook his head. It was a pivotal moment in the match.

Early in the partnership between Kippax and Stan McCabe, 'some of the spectators on the mound began to voice displeasure at the slow batting'. They were hard to please: Kippax, all easy elegance, and the more pugnacious McCabe, added 182 runs to the score in only 132 minutes, wresting the game away from the visitors. Kippax's batting was based on fluid drives and deft late cuts, while McCabe had a muscular back-foot game, pulling and hooking savagely. As the ball became older and softer, and the pitch eased in pace, the West Indian quick bowlers became easier to play, and Tommy Scott and Frank Martin were unable to duplicate the accuracy and control that Grimmett and Hurwood had produced. The temperature rose above 102 degrees, so the faster bowlers could be used only in short spells. McCabe was dropped twice – sharp, difficult chances to Roach and Grant – and he seemed certain to reach his first century in Test cricket until he tried to hook a bouncer from Constantine and skied it to square leg. It was the kind of catch that, ordinarily, a wicket-keeper would claim, but Constantine still had little faith in Ivan Barrow. He called loudly for the ball, sprinted into position, and held it cleanly.

Early on the third day, Australia had reached 341 for five and a massive total appeared likely. But the persistent Herman Griffith removed Kippax and then Tommy Scott 'realized that something had to be done. I felt that we had to make an effort to pull the match around. I went on the field feeling that I could have done anything I wanted with the ball.' Whatever the source of this new confidence may have been, it worked. In only nine balls, Scott removed Oldfield, Grimmett, Hurwood and Wall without conceding a single run. Australia's lead was no more than 80.

It was a significant achievement for the West Indies to dismiss Australia for 376. On tour in England, the Australians had averaged just under 500 runs an innings in the Tests, running up such scores as 729 for six, 695 and 566. Adelaide was notoriously a good pitch for batting, so Grant's team had plenty of reason to be satisfied with their efforts. But they were still behind in the game, and needed to improve on their first innings if they were to set Australia a decent target. They battled hard; Lionel Birkett played beautifully for his half-century, cutting and cover driving fluently. Grant duplicated his dogged resistance from the first innings playing, as George Headley put it, 'with a grim determination that was something to see'. Appearing in his first Test match, Grant became the first cricketer to pass fifty in each innings of a Test without being dismissed.

But the Australians were playing the game on a different level. 'West Indies cricket is quite different to what is played in Australia' George Headley observed. 'There you get no half volleys.' Not only that, but 'their scorer, I found', Learie Constantine recalled, 'had for many years kept a chart of all runs scored by opposing batsmen in all Tests, showing the number, the direction of the hits, the weaknesses of the batsman's play, and so on. Everything is tabulated

Alec Hurwood.

Barto Bartlett.

and indexed, so that, before a Test, the Australian captain has only to consult the records to find every detail or weakness or strength in every opposing player.' After the Adelaide Test, the Australian scorer, Bill Ferguson, showed Headley the chart of his century against Victoria, 'and it showed that most of my runs were scored on the off side'. Clarrie Grimmett was well aware of Headley's strength, so he packed the leg side field and bowled at Headley's leg stump. Denied any opportunity to score, Headley resolved to 'dig in', and he 'played four consecutive maiden overs from Grimmett with a view to breaking the back of their attack. In the fifth over, I realise, Grimmett was getting fed up with my presence at that particular end, and I was getting fed up with him. On the fourth delivery, I tried to drive the ball, missed and was stumped. Once more Oldfield was my executioner; I only made 11.'

When Headley returned to the dressing room, Tommy Scott took him aside. 'Well, George,' he said, 'you are too good a player to be out in that fashion. Grimmett was tiring after bowling so many maiden overs. He kidded you and you fell for it. Good batsman as you are, the bowler must get you out rather than you get yourself out. A good batsman doesn't do things like that, he is better off in the middle.' Headley didn't resent the advice: he knew it was right. He just needed to work out how to put it into practice.

The Australians always seemed to be working to a plan. As Jack Grant blocked away grimly on the third day, Bill Woodfull tossed the ball to Bradman, who sometimes sent down innocent-looking leg breaks. Woodfull remembered that, back in June, the Australians had played against Cambridge University, and Grant had been dismissed by Bradman (who took six wickets in the game) in the second innings. It was worth another try. This time, Grant resisted everything Bradman sent down, but Ivan Barrow, after defending stoutly for 75 minutes, missed a straight ball, and the lbw decision gave Bradman the first of his two wickets in Test cricket.

The Australians were set a target of 172 on the fourth day. It wasn't enough. As Archie Jackson walked out to open the innings with Bill Ponsford, he turned to umpire George Hele and smiled, 'I see the skipper's padded up, but we won't give him a knock.' They didn't. It took just under two and a half hours for the Australians to clinch the game, Jackson ending proceedings by punching a ball from Constantine to the leg-side fence.

Australia v West Indies

Adelaide Oval, 12, 13, 15, 16 December 1930

Umpires: GA Hele, AG Jenkins

Australia won by ten wickets.

West Indies

CA Roach	st Oldfield b Hurwood	56	b Hurwood	9
LS Birkett	c and b Grimmett	27	st Oldfield b Grimmett	64
GA Headley	c Wall b Grimmett	0	st Oldfield b Grimmett	11
FR Martin	b Grimmett	39	run out	3
LN Constantine	c Wall b Grimmett	1	b Grimmett	14
GC Grant	not out	53	not out	71
EL Bartlett	lbw b Grimmett	84	c Grimmett b Hurwood	11
IM Barrow	c Bradman b Grimmett	12	lbw b Bradman	27
GN Francis	lbw b Hurwood	5	b Hurwood	3
OC Scott	c Fairfax b Grimmett	3	c Kippax b Hurwood	8
HC Griffith	b Hurwood	1	st Oldfield b Grimmett	10
Extras	(6 b, 8 lb, 1 nb)	16	(16 b, 2 lb)	18
Total		296		249

Bowling

	Overs	Mdns	Runs	Wkts		Overs	Mdns	Runs	Wkts
Wall	16	-	64	0		10	1	20	0
Fairfax	11	1	36	0		3	2	6	0
Grimmett	48	19	87	7		38	7	96	4
Hurwood	36.1	14	55	3		34	11	86	4
McCabe	12	3	32	0		8	2	15	0
Bradman	4	-	7	0		5	1	8	1

Australia

WH Ponsford	c Birkett b Francis	24	not out	92
A Jackson	c Barrow b Francis	31	not out	70
DG Bradman	c Grant b Griffith	4		
AF Kippax	c Barrow b Griffith	146		
SJ McCabe	c and b Constantine	90		
WM Woodfull	run out	6		
AG Fairfax	not out	41		
WAS Oldfield	c Francis b Scott	6		
CV Grimmett	c Barrow b Scott	0		
A Hurwood	c Martin b Scott	0		
TW Wall	lbw b Scott	0		
Extras	(2 b, 10 lb, 7 nb)	19	(8 b, 1 nb, 1 w)	10
Total		376	(0 wickets)	172

Bowling

	Overs	Mdns	Runs	Wkts		Overs	Mdns	Runs	Wkts
Francis	18	7	43	2		10	1	30	0
Constantine	22	-	89	1		9.3	3	27	0
Griffith	28	4	69	2		10	1	20	0
Martin	29	3	73	0		11	-	28	0
Scott	20.5	2	83	4		13	-	55	0
Birkett	-	-	-	-		2	-	2	0

The New South Wales representatives in the Australian team remained in Adelaide, for a Sheffield Shield match billed as a clash between the country's best bowler, Grimmett, and its leading batsman, Bradman. That kind of challenge usually acted as a spur to Bradman, but it was Grimmett who made an early impression, luring Jack Fingleton into a defensive prod, beating the outside edge, and giving Charlie Walker a neat stumping as the batsman dragged his foot forward. New South Wales lost its first wicket with the score on 24, after which Grimmett's day took a turn for the worse. Archie Jackson, at his most stylish, was joined by Bradman, at his most relentless. In the next 223 minutes, they added 334 runs, before Jackson was well caught near the long-on fence. He'd made 166, matching Bradman run for run, and playing with all his old poise. Bradman batted on, and on, until he was bowled – by Victor Richardson, of all people – just before stumps. Australia's best batsman had scored 258. Keeping the ball on the ground, always, he'd found the boundary 37 times. It was his tenth double-century in Sheffield Shield matches, and he was still only twenty-two years old. Australia's best bowler, at the end of the first day, was left nursing the gruesome figures of one for 120 from 26 overs.

§

It was almost Christmas, so Archie Jackson sent a gift to the secretary of his grade cricket club, Balmain – three bats for use in the club kit. On the Sunday of the Adelaide Test, members of the West Indian team visited orphanages in Adelaide, helping to distribute presents. They were not invited to another big event of the weekend – the annual Christmas Social of the White Australia League.

§

The West Indians recovered from the intensity of the first Test with two relatively undemanding matches against Tasmania. Oscar Wight and Frank de Caires weren't chosen for the first match, at Launceston, but that was entirely their own fault. For reasons that were never explained, they managed to miss the boat that took the rest of the team to the island, and didn't arrive until the second day of the game. If any formal disciplinary action was taken, it isn't recorded: it's likely that Wight and de Caires were protected from formal sanctions by their relatively lofty social standing. But the episode can hardly have helped either man to stake a claim for a Test place.

Instead, Jack Grant took the opportunity to try to play his Test batsmen into form, a decision that backfired when Tasmania reduced the West Indians to 131 for five. In fact, the Tasmanian side included two very capable fast-medium bowlers – Laurie Nash (who was good enough to play two Tests for Australia) and the talented Owen Burrows, so there were few easy runs. Jack Grant dug in to play another defiant defensive innings and then, on the second day of the game, Learie Constantine cut loose.

Constantine went in to face a leg-spinner, Stuart Taylor, who was playing in his first match for his state. After tapping his first ball for a single, Constantine took the slow bowler apart, cracking three boundaries in an over. He hit out at Burrows as well, and after five minutes at the crease, had already reached 24. Nash returned to the attack, and had some success in slowing the rate of scoring: it took Constantine 20 minutes to get to fifty, which he celebrated by carving 17 runs from a single over from Nash. If the ball was full, he smashed it through cover, often getting down on his right knee as he played the stroke; if the ball was short, he hoisted it over mid-wicket. When lunch was taken, Constantine had scored 65 in 25 minutes, and he had failed to score from only two of the deliveries he faced.

During the lunch break, the teams were introduced to the Federal Minister for Works and Railways, Joe Lyons, who was home in Tasmania for the Christmas holiday. A former Premier of Tasmania, Lyons had worked his way out of poverty (initially as a schoolteacher) after his father had squandered all of the family's money betting unsuccessfully on the 1887 Melbourne Cup. Although (or perhaps because) he bore a startling resemblance to the cartoon koala Blinky Bill, Lyons projected an avuncular geniality that made him a formidable candidate in election campaigns. Whether his visit had a sobering effect on Constantine is hard to say, but the batsman's progress after the break was more measured. He reached his hundred – by pulling a ball from Nash into the fence on the full – after batting for 52 minutes, and it hardly mattered that he was bowled by the next ball. He had scored exactly 100 in a partnership of 128 with his captain. Doug Green, the Tasmanian batsman, later said that 'I can only remember one ball he didn't score off. It was too high. Should've been a wide.'

Tasmania collapsed twice, and lost by an innings. They did better in the second game, in Hobart, which, oddly, was scheduled on Christmas Eve,

Christmas Day and Boxing Day. Constantine took wickets, Lionel Birkett and Frank Martin scored freely, and rain on the third day prevented any result. But the visit to Tasmania was deeply frustrating for the two late arrivals, Frank de Caires and Oscar Wight. At least de Caires was given an opportunity at Hobart, where he set about playing a cautious, deliberate innings. Unfortunately, Lionel Birkett then tapped a ball straight to mid on, and set off for a foolhardy single. Answering his partner's call, de Caires was beaten home by the throw: run out for five. Oscar Wight, on the other hand, remained simmering in the pavilion throughout the match, furious at his lack of opportunity. He felt that his cards had been marked. Upon his return home, he complained that 'there was distinct partiality shown throughout the tour and this was decidedly detrimental to the morale of the team... Whether it was done consciously or not, I am not prepared to say but it was done to such an extent as to make others feel that it was not worth trying, save for self-satisfaction. *I know.*'

§

When play finished in Hobart, both teams spent the night together at the Theatre Royal, for the opening night of the stage play, *Dracula*. This was 'a weird and thrilling entertainment', presented by the Alexander Marsh Company, that 'concerns a fictitious but intensely interesting vampire theme.' The play was the hit of the holiday season in Hobart: the *Hobart Mercury* explained that 'the attendances at the Theatre Royal are a sure indication that straightout melodrama, well acted, has the same appeal as in days gone by', and particularly enjoyed the 'shrieks of apprehension in the theatre nightly.' What the West Indians made of it all is not recorded.

§

Rain destroyed the annual Christmas match between Victoria and New South Wales in Melbourne. Only a few overs were bowled on the first three days, and there wasn't even time for a result on the first innings. Yet the game produced two exceptional innings. Bill Ponsford batted all the way through Victoria's innings, remaining unbeaten on 109 in a total of 185. On a dreadful pitch, he placed the ball deftly and monopolised the strike when batting with the tail, yet still played aggressively whenever offered something loose. Bert Ironmonger and Don Blackie had the use of a helpful surface, and enough time to dismiss New South Wales at least once. Bradman, Kippax, McCabe and Fairfax all went cheaply, but the Victorians were held up by Archie Jackson. This was something new from Jackson: a long, careful, essentially defensive innings. For two and a half hours, he defied the attack as wickets fell around him; when play ended, he was still at the crease, having scored 52 out of his side's 97 for six.

In accordance with a long and strange tradition, play in the Sheffield Shield match in Adelaide began on Christmas day. With no Bradman to bother him, Clarrie Grimmett twice bowled Queensland out cheaply, and the visitors suffered a humbling defeat. But the stalemate in Melbourne meant that Queensland could still win its first Sheffield Shield, if it could defeat Victoria at home in its final match.

§

The Australian Board of Control met in Melbourne on 30 December, and summoned Don Bradman to explain why he should not be sanctioned for a breach of his tour contract in England. There had been a provision in every player's contract stipulating that 'Neither the manager, treasurer, nor any player shall accept employment as a newspaper correspondent or do any work for or in connection with any newspaper or any broadcasting, and no member of the team other than the manager shall directly or indirectly, in any capacity whatever, communicate with the Press nor give any information concerning matters connected with the tour to the Press or to any other servant or agent thereof.' Bradman has allowed an English newspaper to publish his autobiography, in serial form, while the tour was in progress, and the Board argued that this was a breach of his contract.

Bradman protested that there had been no breach of contract. He had not been employed as a newspaper correspondent, had not done work for a newspaper and had not communicated with the press in relation to the tour – his autobiography ended before the tour began. In any case, his publisher had paid him, before the tour, a lump sum for his autobiography, which included serialisation rights – so it had been the publisher who sold the book to the papers, not Bradman. Besides, while the tour was in progress, Clarrie Grimmett's serialised book appeared in several Australian newspapers, and no one had objected to that.

If the matter had ever been pursued through a court, Bradman would almost certainly have won, since he hadn't contravened either the strict terms of the contract, or its obvious purpose, which was to prevent players from talking to the press about the tour. But the Board was both prosecutor and judge, so the outcome was not in doubt. Unanimously, the Board decided that Bradman had breached his contract. He was censured, and £50 was withheld from his final tour payment. Bill Jeanes, the Secretary of the Board, issued a magnificently pompous and meaningless statement, saying that 'the board took into serious consideration its obligations in the control and regulation of the game, and took cognisance of what had occurred'.

The 1930 Australian tour to England produced a record profit of £21,000 for the Board of Control, all from takings at the gate, and it was impossible to deny that much of the huge public interest in the tour was generated by Bradman. Especially in that context, the Board's decision to fine him for a non-existent breach of contract was extraordinarily petty, but ultimately it had nothing much to do with the terms of the tour agreement. It was a reminder to Bradman that no matter how many runs he made, he was still just a player, and he should know his place.

Bradman, at last, had something to say to the press. 'I am very tired', he smiled, 'and it has been hard work playing cricket since I came back. In Adelaide I just felt that I had to put my mind to it to force myself to concentrate. The board has decided that I broke the agreement. I do not think I did. I never saw a newspaper man in England. I certainly wrote a book, and the agreement did not forbid that. However, it is over and that's all there is to say about it. I do not want to think any more about it.'

Australia v West Indies

Sydney Cricket Ground, 1, 2, 3, 5 January 1931

Umpires: GE Borwick, WG French

Australia won by an innings and 172 runs

Australia

WH Ponsford	b Scott	183
A Jackson	c Francis b Griffith	8
DG Bradman	c Barrow b Francis	25
AF Kippax	c Bartlett b Griffith	10
SJ McCabe	lbw b Scott	31
WM Woodfull	c Barrow b Constantine	58
AG Fairfax	c Constantine b Francis	15
WAS Oldfield	run out	0
CV Grimmett	b Scott	12
A Hurwood	c Martin b Scott	5
H Ironmonger	not out	3
Extras	(6 b, 5 lb, 3 nb, 5 w)	19
Total		369

Bowling

	Overs	Mdns	Runs	Wkts
Griffith	28	4	57	2
Constantine	18	2	56	1
Francis	27	3	70	2
Scott	15.4	-	66	4
Martin	18	1	60	0
Birkett	10	1	41	0

West Indies

CA Roach	run out	7	c Kippax b McCabe	25
LS Birkett	c Hurwood b Fairfax	3	c McCabe b Hurwood	8
GA Headley	b Fairfax	14	c Jackson b Hurwood	2
FR Martin	lbw b Grimmett	10	c McCabe b Hurwood	0
GC Grant	c Hurwood b Ironmonger	6	not out	15
LN Constantine	c Bradman b Grimmett	12	b Hurwood	8
IM Barrow	c Jackson b Fairfax	17	c McCabe b Ironmonger	10
GN Francis	b Grimmett	8	c Oldfield b Ironmonger	0
OC Scott	not out	15	c Woodfull b Ironmonger	17
HC Griffith	c Kippax b Grimmett	9	lbw b Grimmett	0
EL Bartlett	absent hurt	-	absent hurt	-
Extras	(6 b, 1 nb)	7	(1 b, 2 lb, 1 nb, 1 w)	5
Total		107		90

Bowling

	Overs	Mdns	Runs	Wkts		Overs	Mdns	Runs	Wkts
Fairfax	13	4	19	3		5	1	21	0
Hurwood	5	1	7	0		11	2	22	4
Grimmett	19.1	2	54	4		3.3	1	9	1
Ironmonger	13	3	20	1		4	1	13	3
McCabe						7	-	20	1

6

January

George Headley finds an answer; Prime Minister Scullin comes home; Archie Jackson is unwell; Bert Ironmonger is in two places at once; and Queensland cricket self-sabotages.

For the second Test, which began in Sydney on New Year's Day, 1931, the Australian selectors made one small, but ominous, change to their team. Tim Wall, the fastest and least successful of the Australian bowlers in Adelaide, was dropped to make room for Bert Ironmonger. The home team went into the game with three spinners, while the visitors' attack was still based on pace.

This time, Australia batted first, and its first innings was oddly similar to its first effort in Adelaide. Again, they started poorly, and Bradman failed, reaching 25 before he edged a ball from Francis to Barrow behind the stumps. Archie Jackson failed, too, edging Griffith to slip where Francis held a catch that was, according to one newspaper, 'so brilliant that Grant, the captain, walked across and patted him heartily on the back.' Australia was 69 for three when Kippax cracked a fierce drive to mid-on, only for Bartlett to take a brilliant diving catch. In the process, however, the fieldsman broke a finger on his right hand, and he took no further part in the game. Then, as in Adelaide, the innings was redeemed by one player constructing a big hundred. This time it was Ponsford, who batted through the whole of the first day, contributing 174 to the total of 323 for four. 'Some in Australia believe that Ponsford is a better bat than Bradman', Ivan Barrow later observed, 'and our bowlers too were almost inclined to think so – Ponsford has a very sound defence and can punish a bowler mercilessly if he loses his length at all.' Some of the crowd thought his innings was a touch slow – when Ponsford had reached about 120, and showed no signs of accelerating, one barracker called out, 'Do you think you've got your eye in yet?'

The West Indies had an early opportunity to remove Ponsford who, Jack Grant recalled, 'played forward to Francis and touched the ball. It flew to me at second slip and I dropped it. I confess that for the barest fraction of a second my mind was not fully on the ball. I was wondering whether to take Francis off and who to put on in his place. It was at that very fraction of a second that the ball came to me.' Otherwise, the West Indians bowled and fielded well, but the pitch was painfully slow. At the end of play, the great fast bowler Jack Gregory visited the West Indian dressing room and told Constantine that 'if they'd given me pitches like this to bowl on, I'd have gone in for tennis!'

The pitch was left uncovered overnight, and it was drenched by rain so heavy that the whole of the second day's play was washed out. Play resumed on the third morning in bright sunshine, and the drying pitch became increasingly treacherous. Australia's last six wickets added only 46 more runs; as in Adelaide, Tommy Scott made short work of the tail. Ponsford gave George Headley an opportunity to show that Constantine wasn't the only fine fieldsman in the West Indies side; the Australian tapped a ball towards cover and ran, but Headley sprinted to the ball, gathered and threw it almost in a single motion, and hit the stumps with Oldfield yards from safety. There was a moment of comedy at the end of the innings, when Bert Ironmonger ambled to the crease and Jack Grant, studiously and diligently, began to rearrange his field. This greatly amused the crowd, who understood that there was only a tiny chance of Ironmonger making contact with the ball, and no telling where it might go if he managed to connect.

By the time the West Indians began their innings, the ball was spitting unpredictably from the pitch. Alan Fairfax found awkward bounce, and jagged the ball off the seam, drawing a false stroke from Headley, who chopped the ball into his stumps. Constantine tried to hit his way out of trouble against Grimmett, only to find Bradman, waiting for the catch right against the midwicket fence. In just over two hours, the West Indies were dismissed for only 107. Woodfull enforced the follow-on, and Alec Hurwood produced the most memorable spell of his international career, removing Birkett, Headley and Martin without conceding a run. The West Indies limped to 67 for five at stumps, and although the pitch had eased by the following morning, it was too late to make any difference.

Learie Constantine in the Sydney Cricket Ground nets.

Prime Minister James Scullin (left) and NSW Premier, Jack Lang (right).

Hurwood ended the innings with four cheap wickets. In his two Tests, he'd taken eleven wickets at an average of fifteen. After all the frustration he'd suffered in England, his position in the Test side now looked surprisingly secure.

§

When the Sydney Test ended early on the fourth scheduled day, the West Indies team remained at the Sydney Cricket Ground. They had a quick lunch, and then went back out onto the field for practice. 'A cynical imp on my shoulder', Arthur Mailey wrote, 'suggests that after their Test showing they needed the practice. That may be so. Still, I have seen other teams beaten just as hopelessly as were the visitors, drift sadly away from the ground as though there was nothing left in life. We must admire the West Indies players for this spirit and that which they have infused into cricket during their stay here.'

George Headley had failed four times in as many Test innings, and was looking for answers. Oscar Wight thought that he had identified the problem, insisting that 'I attribute Headley's run of "bad luck" to a loss of confidence wholly due to a jealousy brought about by his wonderful success which placed him in competition as a drawing card. Far-fetched though this may seem, there is more in it than will ever be known and it was obvious wherein the root of the evil existed, but there are none so blind as those who will not see.' It was Constantine's fault, in other words.

Was Constantine jealous of Headley's success? It's possible – he was accustomed to being the focus of attention in the West Indies team, and he enjoyed it. On the other hand, Constantine received no shortage of attention in Australia, and the two men maintained a cordial relationship (based more on mutual respect than personal warmth) throughout their lives. If Headley ever did have a problem with Constantine, he never gave voice to it. He saw his problem in purely technical terms. He was essentially a side-on, off-side player, but now 'I discovered that I was being attacked on or about my leg stump, by all their bowlers, necessitating changing my batting technique to combat their guile.' So he decided to adopt 'a new stance, a two-eyed stance to combat the leg side field.' ' In his new stance, Headley kept his front foot in the same position as before, but moved his back foot several inches across to the off side. This had the effect of opening up his right shoulder so that his body was significantly more square-on to the bowler. He found that 'it gave me such command that I could now punch the ball through the leg side field.' The West Indies team had no technical advisor and nothing resembling a coach: Headley had arrived at this solution by himself. By the end of the tour, Grimmett was describing Headley as the best on-side player he had ever seen.

§

Journalists began to ask whether the West Indians were up to the standards required by Test cricket – some more trenchantly than others. 'Unfortunately,' grumbled the *Labor Daily*, 'the West Indians still have to play in three more Tests. The side should never have been allowed more than three international fixtures. Apart from Constantine, not one member of the side could get a place in a New South Wales XI. Birkett and Grant certainly couldn't find a place in a Second XI of the State and Martin, portly veteran, wouldn't get a game with Paddington in first grade cricket.'

Other journalists proposed that the Test selectors should use the remaining matches to give opportunities to promising young players. Keith Rigg, who had been twelfth man in the first two Tests, was often mentioned, as were Jack Nitschke from South Australia and left-arm spinner Bill Hunt of New South Wales. No one took the idea very seriously. There was an issue of principle at stake – that the best side should be chosen for every Test – and also a very practical concern, that the regular Test players had no intention of giving up their £30 match fees. The average weekly wage for an adult male in Australia in 1930 was just over £5, so Test cricketers were very comfortably rewarded. 'This £30 is easy money', one of the players told Arthur Mailey, 'and, personally, I don't wish to be deprived of it simply because I happen to be in the winning team.'

§

The day after the second Test ended, so did the steel fabrication work for the Sydney Harbour Bridge. The 150 men who had been working the night shift were informed that their services were no longer required.

§

Back in Brisbane after his triumph in the Sydney Test, Alec Hurwood was looking forward to playing his first Test in his home city. Instead, he was called into a meeting at General Motors, where he worked as an accountant. The firm had been happy to give him leave to make the tour to England, but he had now been away from his desk for almost a year. How much more work did he intend to miss for cricket? There was a Depression, cars were a luxury, sales were down, and Brisbane was full of unemployed accountants eager to turn up to work every day. Politely but firmly, Hurwood was told: make a choice.

The following day, Hurwood informed the Test selectors that he was unavailable for the rest of the series. He didn't play another first-class match for the rest of the season. He never played another Test.

§

Prime Minister Jim Scullin returned from the Imperial Conference in London, reaching Fremantle in early January. Upon his arrival, he addressed a large public gathering, saying: 'When I hear people say, "We are looking to the return of the Prime Minister, for he will lift Australia out of its present difficulties", I feel that I have grave limitations. Governments have their limitations, and no man nor any group of men in Australia could lift Australia out of her difficulties. It will require strong and united effort if Australia is to get on to the high road to prosperity.'

This was strikingly candid and honest. It also sounded very much like an admission of defeat.

§

Eddie Gilbert was bowling fast. He'd already dismissed Frank Martin and Lionel Birkett by the time Learie Constantine came to the crease, and the match between Queensland and the West Indies was evenly balanced. Gilbert had been told that Constantine was a ferocious driver of the ball, so he decided to try him out with a bouncer. Constantine cracked the ball to square leg for four. Gilbert tried again, shorter and faster, and this time Constantine made meaty contact, sending the ball high over mid-wicket for six. And Gilbert responded by smiling, walking down the pitch, and shaking Constantine by the hand. 'No one', he said, 'has ever done that to me before.'

Between Gilbert and Constantine, honours ended up more or less even. Gilbert was easily the best of the Queensland bowlers: he dismissed Grant, Sealy and Scott to claim 5-65 in the first innings, and held a brilliant diving catch to remove Birkett in the second innings, when he also took two cheap wickets before a shoulder injury forced him out of the attack. It was the most successful performance any Australian fast bowler produced against the tourists. Constantine found that Gilbert was 'the only very fast bowler I have known who begins the over at a clinking good speed and gets faster every ball'.

But Constantine again showed what an exceptional performer he could be. He not only top-scored twice, with 75 and 97, but also had the best bowling figures in each innings, claiming seven wickets in all. He was also far and away the most entertaining player on the field. It took him only 146 minutes to score his 172 runs, his fielding was extraordinary and his bowling rapid. In the first innings, he scored 47 of the first fifty runs in a partnership with Derek Sealy, cracking 17 from a single over from Vic Goodwin. He simply powered his team to a morale-boosting victory, by the substantial margin of 219 runs. 'Constantine was always in the picture', according to one Brisbane reporter. 'He seems to be everywhere. If he is fielding at mid-on he races like a greyhound to the leg boundary, when a ball goes that way, and yet he is just as much in evidence when some backing up is to be done at the bowler's end. Some of his picking up and throwing in, done with the one action, was astonishing. One return of a very fast shot in the slips was a gem. He returned it straight to the bowler in a twinkling without even having turned round.'

The result would have been even more emphatic but for some disciplined, courageous batting by Vic Goodwin. Goodwin had been omitted from the team when it was first announced, even though he had topped the batting averages on Queensland's southern tour. This made no obvious sense, and there were some heavy hints that he was being punished for his role in the rebellious team meeting in Sydney. Then Cecil Thompson withdrew from the side with an injury, and Goodwin was reprieved. There was nothing very exciting about his two innings, which were slow and watchful, but each time he was battling to arrest an early collapse. It may not have been

Constantine-class entertainment, but his scores of 60 and 54 were a pointed rebuke to the selectors.

§

By early 1931, thousands of families in Australia were entirely dependent upon government sustenance – the 'susso'. Australia had no coherent national policy on welfare, and sustenance was left to the state governments, so it varied from time to time and from place to place. Usually the susso took the form of vouchers or coupons exchangeable for food; sometimes men were required to work for it; often it was accompanied by demeaning and humiliating processes and paperwork. The Queensland government paid more than Victoria: in early 1931, it increased sustenance payments to seventeen shillings a week for a single man (Victoria paid only five). A married couple with eight children received three pounds, nine shillings and sixpence a week in Queensland, but just over a pound in Victoria. But that didn't mean that Queensland was more generous: it had the lowest proportion of unemployed men anywhere in the country, and it imposed the most stringent requirements on sustenance recipients, who effectively needed to be incapacitated in order to qualify. In Tasmania, men were put to work on public projects in exchange for ration cards, and those with the larger families worked longer hours, since they were given more rations. Western Australia was the only State that allowed any portion of sustenance to be paid in cash.

And still unemployment continued to rise. Early in 1931, 29% of union members were unemployed in South Australia, 27% in Tasmania and 27% in New South Wales.

The South Australian government had, notoriously, one of the stingiest sustenance programs in the country. A family that would receive 35 shillings a week in Western Australia was given rations worth 18 shillings and ninepence in South Australia. In January, the South Australian government announced that it was withdrawing beef from the sustenance ration, replacing it with mutton or sausages. The weekly ration also included (for two adults) three loaves of bread, a pound of sugar, three and a half ounces of tea, eight ounces of rice and oatmeal, a tin of jam, two ounces of raisins and a tin of condensed milk.

On 10 January, two thousand unemployed men gathered at the Waterside Workers' Hall in Port Adelaide to march to the city in protest against their loss of beef. As the march drew closer to the city, it grew stronger, swelling with ragged, hungry, angry men. Along with signs demanding beef, the protesters carried placards reading 'Down with Imperialism'. Police on horseback and motorcycles accompanied the march, their numbers growing larger, too, as the protesters entered the centre of the city.

The idea was that, once the march reached the Treasury building in King William Street, a delegation of six men would go inside to speak with members of the State government. The marchers waited at the doors of Treasury for about half an hour, the mood becoming angrier all the time. And then the doors opened to reveal, not politicians, but more police.

It isn't clear how the fighting started. The police later claimed that the marchers had started using their placards as weapons; the marchers accused the police of using their batons too aggressively. However it began, the march disintegrated into a violent riot. No guns were used, but for twenty minutes, men swung batons, signs and fists. Police on horseback and motorcycles drove indiscriminately into the crowd. There were no fatalities, but twelve arrests were made and seventeen men were admitted to hospital. Sleepy, conservative Adelaide had become the scene of the most violent civil unrest in Australia during the Depression – the Beef Riot.

§

The Brisbane Test match was finished as a contest within a couple of hours. In the very first over of the game, George Francis removed Archie Jackson for a first-ball duck, but that only served to bring Bill Ponsford and Don Bradman together, and their partnership of 230 (in only 163 minutes) took the game well beyond the reach of the West Indies.

It could have been very different. Learie Constantine generated plenty of pace and bounce with the new ball, and he thought that Bradman 'did not care very much for speed bowling when there were good fielders in the slips. I think he got over this later, but at the time there was no doubt about it. So we put our heads together in the pavilion, and when he came to the wicket, I arranged my field with the greatest care... I bowled carefully, to lull him into security without ever showing what was coming.Then, when we had more or less let him get four runs, I gave him one or two balls as bait, and then shot down my fastest on his off stump breaking away. He put it straight into first slip's hands and first slip dropped it.' There are however, newspaper reports that insist that the ball flew, at a comfortable height, directly between the fieldsmen at second and third slips, each of whom left it for the other, although it was probably Birkett's catch. Either way, Bradman gave Constantine 'one look, as much as to say that he saw it all, and then settled down grimly.'

It was another unlucky day for Constantine, who also had Ponsford and Kippax dropped, and it was not Bradman's habit to waste a bit of good fortune. At the end of the day, he was unbeaten on 223 – a new record for an Australian batsman in a Test in Australia. Most of his runs came through the on-side; he pillaged the bowling of Tommy Scott, who was a little too slow for the pitch, allowing Bradman to step right back and punch the ball through the gaps in the leg-side field. 'Bradman is a genius', Scott admitted. 'He looks for his openings and hits the ball through them keeping it low. The balls from his bat all travel along the ground. He is a very clever batsman and hits with great precision.' Scott played seven matches against Bradman during the tour, but never managed to capture his wicket.

Nor did the faster bowlers trouble Bradman much; when they attacked his leg stump, he glanced them away behind square leg; when they adjusted their line, he drove them straight back down the ground. The score mounted rapidly; Bradman and Kippax raised a century partnership in only 66 minutes, and it took only 46 minutes to carry the team's total from 300 to 400. Australia plundered 428 runs on the first day, losing only three wickets. The only bowler to contain the scoring effectively was Lionel Birkett, a very occasional off-spinner, who even managed to snare his only Test wicket, bowling Kippax with a delivery that skidded through low. The West Indians never gave up, fielding enthusiastically and bowling energetically, but there was no way for them to get back into the game.

Writing after the match, Bradman concluded that, although the West Indian attack 'was reasonably strong (and too much praise cannot be given to the three fast bowlers for the way they stood up to their work), Scott was scarcely up to international standard as a slow bowler, and Martin's left-hand bowling was not quite class enough to make him a stock bowler.' It was a fair comment, at least based on the game in Brisbane, where Scott and Martin took one horribly expensive wicket between them from 51 overs. At least Constantine had a moment to relish at the start of the second day; he gave Bradman a bouncer, and the mis-timed pull looped to Jack Grant at square leg. Bradman hadn't added a run to his overnight score.

The West Indies' reply stuttered against Grimmett, Ironmonger and Ron Oxenham, who had replaced Alec Hurwood in the Australian attack. The exception was George Headley, whose new method worked more effectively than he had dared to hope. It wasn't his brightest effort; for long stretches of time, he simply concentrated on preserving his wicket against some impressively accurate bowling. But Tommy Scott's advice resonated with him: there was no reason for him to throw away his wicket, merely because he had just played out a few maidens. After batting for two hours, he had scored only 21 runs. His patience, now, was stronger than Grimmett's; when the leg-spinner eventually tried something different, Headley cracked him for two fours in succession, with a fierce cut and a pull.

At around this stage of the game, Oscar Wight made his first appearance on the field during a Test match. Archie Jackson began to feel unwell, and left the field to rest. But the Australian twelfth man, Keith Rigg, was already on the ground. Bill Ponsford had spent the rest day on a boat, happily fishing on Moreton Bay, kicking off his shoes and rolling up his trousers. By the time the boat returned to shore, his feet were so badly sunburned that he couldn't field for the next two days. Jackson's illness left the Australians with ten fit men, so Grant obligingly lent Wight to them as a substitute.

Jack Grant and Learie Constantine were dismissed in quick succession, but Headley carried on, hitting Ironmonger for three boundaries in an over: a drive over mid-off, a late cut and a square cut. Headley was delighted to find that his new stance didn't prevent him from striking the ball cleanly through the off side when the opportunity presented itself. Ivan Barrow stuck with him for almost an hour; the wicket-keeper had made no large scores in the series, but developed the habit of contributing handy small ones. By the time Grimmett tempted Barrow out of his crease, Headley was within sight of his century – which he reached a couple of overs later, stroking Grimmett through the on side for two. He was still batting, on 102, when the innings closed a few minutes later. His ten team-mates mustered 88 runs between them.

Headley's innings received only muted praise from the Australian press. 'It was pathetic', according to *The Referee,* 'to see a batsman of Headley's ability taking 104 minutes to score 19 runs'. The *Brisbane Courier* argued that 'Headley has been compared with Bradman, but he is a player of an entirely different type. Sound in defence, he was seldom worried by the bowlers, but at no time did he attempt to force the pace. His best shots were those to square leg, behind point, and a forcing shot to the on. While his placing was all right, he has neither the versatility nor the freedom of stroke play of Bradman, nor has he the daring and ability to score from good length bowling.' None of this bothered Headley, who thought that 'the century I scored was one of the best that I made in any Test match.' He celebrated by returning to the team's hotel at the end of the day, smoking a cigarette and playing a game of bridge.

Headley was batting again before long: the West Indians followed on, and Clifford Roach lasted only a few overs. This time, Headley was more positive and confident, and played with greater aggression. He moved to 28 in quick time. As the field changed between overs, Stan McCabe passed him, and commented, 'Gee, George, you're going to get another hundred against us!' McCabe was a genuinely affable man, and he meant well, but his remark disturbed Headley's concentration. He began to think about the next century, rather than the next ball – a harmless delivery, down the leg side, from Ironmonger, which Headley glanced straight into Bert Oldfield's gloves. The match ended, and the series was decided, early on the fourth day.

§

Bert Ironmonger performed the unusual feat of appearing in two matches, over a thousand miles apart, simultaneously. His grade club, St Kilda, chose him for a game against Prahran, scheduled for two successive Saturdays, even though the selectors knew that he would be in Brisbane for the Test on the second day of the match. The reasoning appears to have been that his bowling would be valuable on the first day, while his batting wouldn't be missed on the second.

It didn't end well. Prahran ran up a total of 275 and, although Don Blackie and 'Chuck' Fleetwood-Smith shared seven victims, Ironmonger conceded 92 runs without taking a single wicket – the worst return of his long career in Pennant cricket. On the second day, St Kilda's chase fell 29 runs short, when Fleetwood-Smith was bowled one minute before the scheduled time for close of play. That was the ninth wicket to fall, and the umpires walked from the field and ruled the match a draw, saying that there had been insufficient time for the last batsman to begin his innings. The Prahran players protested that the last batsman couldn't have commenced his innings under any circumstances, because everyone knew that he was in Brisbane. Prahran appealed to the Victorian Cricket Association, arguing that Ironmonger should have been listed as absent, so that the innings closed when Fleetwood-Smith was dismissed. The appeal was rejected, and the result was confirmed as a draw.

§

The third Test began on a Friday, and the Sunday, as always, was a rest day. A Sunday school teacher was leaving her church in the northern Brisbane suburb of Sandgate when two black men arrived on its doorstep, raised their hats, and asked to look inside. The organist was still playing when they entered the church, and was surprised when the taller man began to sing along in a deep, rich voice. It was Clifford Roach, who was taking in the sights of Brisbane with Eddie Gilbert.

Roach and Gilbert weren't the only pair of cricketers to visit a church in Brisbane. The Central Methodist Mission entertained a visit from Jack Grant and Bill Woodfull. The 1930-31 Test series was the only one ever to be played in Australia between teams led by non-drinking, regular churchgoers. Woodfull's faith may not have been as obviously zealous as Grant's but it was dutiful – the son of a Methodist minister, he was a Sabbath-observing teetotaller. He explained to the gathering that he felt quite at home at the Mission, since his father had been the superintendent of the equivalent mission in Melbourne for several years. Asked to tell the meeting something about the West Indies, Grant responded that he would 'not launch into a description of the industries and physical features of my homeland, but I will content myself by drawing attention to one striking feature of our social life. Many a stranger coming to our shores has been struck by the fact that there people of different colour and different creeds live contentedly and peacefully together. We all worship together, we play together, and we attend the same schools. This may seem strange to you but with us it seems quite natural.'

That was true, but not the whole truth. Each colony in the West Indies had its own caste and class system, and opportunities were not distributed evenly. In Grant's home, Trinidad, each of the major cricket clubs tended to self-segregate to some degree, so that, as the writer CLR James explained, members of

George Francis in the nets.

Jack Grant.

Queen's Park tended to be 'at least part white and often wealthy', while Shamrock was 'the club of the old Catholic families' and 'almost exclusively white'. Maple, where Clifford Roach played, was 'the club of the brown-skinned middle class', while Shannon, where James played alongside Constantine, was 'the club of the black lower middle class'. Black working class men played for Stingo. Something similar occurred in the other West Indian colonies – Herman Griffith, for example, had been one of the founders of the Empire Club in Barbados after black men of his status were excluded from the Spartan Club. Yet these divisions, James thought, didn't harm the development of cricket in the West Indies – rather, they 'sharpened' it, because on the cricket field a man could prove that the extent of his achievements need not be determined by the circumstances of his birth. In particular, James thought, the men at Shannon played with 'pride and impersonal ambition… as if they knew that their club represented the great mass of black people on the island.'

§

George Headley's dismissal in the second innings of the Brisbane Test had been a trap: Ironmonger had deliberately tempted him with a harmless delivery just outside leg stump, and by the time he released the ball, Oldfield was already in position waiting for Headley's stroke. It didn't happen again: as Headley told CLR James, 'I cut that out.'

> 'What do you mean you cut it out?'
>
> 'I just made up my mind never to be caught that way again.'
>
> 'So you do not glance?'
>
> 'Sure I glance, but I take care to find out first if any of these traps are being laid.'
>
> 'Always?'
>
> 'Always.'

§

Archie Jackson fielded on the last morning of the third Test, and then he was ordered to rest. He was named in the New South Wales team to play Victoria in the week after the Test, but he withdrew when a doctor in Sydney told him that he was suffering from influenza.

It wasn't a completely terrible diagnosis: at least the doctor managed to identify that the source of the problem was in Jackson's lungs. It's not certain when or where Jackson contracted tuberculosis, a bacterial infection which can have a long latency period. But it's clear that, during the summer of 1930-31, he was affected by at least the early symptoms of the disease – intermittent tiredness and fever. Later, it became commonplace for people to assert that he had been infected while on tour in England, but there's no real evidence to support that, and throughout the 1920s and 1930s, around three thousand Australians died from tuberculosis each year, so the infection was not uncommon in Australia. Its victims were often unaware that they had the disease until they began to exhibit its most distinctive symptom – coughing up blood – and no one knows for certain when Jackson was diagnosed accurately. It may not have made much difference if the real nature of his illness had been identified earlier, since effective antibiotic treatments for the disease were not developed until another ten years had passed. Tuberculosis wasn't always fatal – sometimes the infection was confined to a single lung, and sometimes the victim's immune system rallied – but there was no cure. The Sydney Anti-Tuberculosis Association had recently announced its plans to 'continue to preach health, encourage people to enjoy the wonderful sunshine, to dress more rationally and to discourage the habit of cocktail drinking amongst the young women', but these were not remedies that offered Jackson any real hope.

§

The West Indian fast bowlers had shared eight wickets in Australia's innings in Brisbane, but it had taken them hours of hard toil. Although their bowling figures were uninspiring, they were widely admired as the best fast bowling combination ever to tour Australia. In part, this was because no touring side had ever before regularly fielded three fast to fast-medium bowlers in the same side. Before the War, convention had dictated that a team should never play more than one fast bowler, the single possible exception being the England team of 1911-12, in which the new ball was shared between Johnny Douglas, Frank Foster and Sydney Barnes (all of whom operated at gradations of brisk medium pace). After the War, Warwick Armstrong had used Jack Gregory and Ted McDonald together, to devestating effect, but few teams could boast bowlers of that calibre, so the experiment was seldom repeated.

At the end of the tour, Frank Martin stated that George Francis had been the most consistent of his team's bowlers. The old Australian captain, Clem Hill, agreed that 'Francis was the best of them.' Francis was tireless, and willing, and dismissed Bradman twice. When the ball was new, he could occasionally move it away from the right-handers; as it aged, his most effective variation was an off-cutter. He had a bouncer, which he employed sparingly, as a surprise weapon. But mostly what he did was plug away, over after over, on a perfect length somewhere near the off stump. Griffith's approach was similar: he had a little more pace than Francis, and a little less variety, although every so often he sent down a slower ball with a leg-break action. He often bowled with dreadful luck, beating the edge or shaving the stumps repeatedly. And, like Francis and Constantine, he suffered from fallible catching behind the wicket. Constantine's bowling lacked the discipline and control of Francis and Griffith: he bowled – at his quickest – faster than either, and he had an extraordinary range of variations. But it often appeared as though he wanted to work through his entire repertoire in a single over, rather than building up pressure through a more patient approach.

Midway through the tour, the old Australian captain Monty Noble visited the West Indies dressing room, and asked bluntly, 'What is wrong with you fellows? You seem unable to play the way we feel you can play.' George Headley replied that 'on these wickets the dice are loaded against us.' The West Indians believed that the Australian pitches had been prepared, deliberately, to favour the home side's spinners. Arguably, this was true of the Melbourne Cricket Ground, where the Victorian team had relied for many years on the slow bowling of Ironmonger and Blackie – Ironmonger's first-class bowling average in Melbourne was 20, half what it was in Sydney. Frank Martin insisted that 'the Melbourne wicket is not like other wickets – they have their own way of preparing it.' Elsewhere, it's fairer to say that Australia had plenty of spinners because the pitches were slow, and those bowlers adapted to the conditions they were given.

Twenty years later, on their next visit to the country, the West Indians arrived in Australia with the world's most potent spin attack, only to discover spicy pitches ideally suited to the pace of Ray Lindwall and Keith Miller.

§

If you lived in Australia in January 1931, and you had a job, you were lucky – but not too lucky. On 22 January, the Commonwealth Court of Conciliation and Arbitration reduced the basic wage by 10%.

§

The executive committee of the Queensland Cricket Association summoned the members of their Sheffield Shield team to a meeting, asking them to 'to show cause why they should not be dealt with for disobedience of instructions from the State selectors and from the executive'. The players held a meeting beforehand, and agreed not to compromise – although they made an exception for Ron Oxenham. Oxenham had just won back his Test place, and had done well in Brisbane, taking seven wickets and scoring useful runs. If the QCA suspended him, he couldn't play for Australia, which would mean the loss of valuable match fees. He was already thirty-nine years old; he wouldn't have many more opportunities. His team-mates agreed that he should apologise to the QCA, and avoid any sanction.

The others stood firm. They didn't deny that they had disobeyed instructions when they appointed their own selectors – instead, they insisted, the instructions were an unjustified departure from the usual, and proper, practice. Cecil Thompson, a schoolteacher, provided a scathing assessment of the executive, in which he wrote that 'I had looked forward with some interest to reading the report of the Q.C.A. selection committee on my return to Brisbane. I had expected some plausible explanation of an action that made the selection committee the laughing stock of all first-class cricketers that we had met in the South and of cricket enthusiasts throughout Australia. However, I was doomed to disappointment. I found a distorted account of events, and, worse still, I found that the selectors had made personal attacks on players, had divulged confidences, and had given snippets of confidential talks. Nowhere could I find any justification for their action.'

Queensland had one match left in its Sheffield Shield season, against Victoria in Brisbane. If Queensland won, it would be back on top of the table, with a strong lead over Victoria, which would then need to win its last match, in Adelaide, outright. Already, the team was weakened by the loss of Alec Hurwood and Eddie Gilbert, who was ruled unfit by a doctor at the Barambah mission. Now, the executive of the QCA resolved that Frank Gough, Cecil Thompson, Mo Biggs, Vic Goodwin, Pud Thurlow, Eric Bensted and Gordon Amos were suspended, and would not be considered for selection in the match against Victoria. Les Gill, who was 39 and hadn't played for Queensland for three years, was recalled as captain, but only after one of the selectors, James Holdsworth, declared himself unavailable for the post. Holdsworth was forty, and had never played for Queensland. Gordon Bourne, in solidarity with the suspended cricketers, promptly made himself unavailable for the game, and several others soon followed his lead. The composition of the team changed almost daily in the week before the match.

Somehow, the QCA had come to the conclusion that keeping the players in their place was more important than winning the Sheffield Shield – an attitude which may explain, in part, why Queensland didn't win the Shield until 1995.

§

Learie Constantine failed twice with the bat in the Brisbane Test. He hadn't yet worked out a method for scoring runs against Australia's attack and, unlike Headley, he never did. Yet he remained an utterly dominant cricketer whenever the opposition was just below top-class. At Newcastle, the New South Wales Country team fielded a decent attack, including one man (Ernie O'Brien) who had played for the State, and two others (fast bowler Leo McGuirk and the leg-spinning all-rounder Albert Bennett) who soon would. The Country combination did well to score 251, and had the West Indians in trouble at 115 for four. Given the chance to open the innings, and anxious to make a good impression, Errol Hunte edged a ball hard into his pads, only to be given out lbw – a decision so obviously unjust that even the parochial crowd cried out for a 'fair go'. Constantine went to the crease early on the second day, and didn't last until the lunch break, but it didn't matter – in only 93 minutes, he thrashed 147runs from 89 deliveries. His six sixes included three successive blows from the leg-spinner O'Brien, the last two of which landed in the street, and he also belted 14 fours. He recalled that the crowd kept urging him to 'break Sutcliffe's record! 132 before lunch!' – a feat he surpassed by 15 runs, although it's far from clear what 'Sutcliffe's record' actually was.

Constantine wasn't done: later that afternoon, he cut through the Country team's second innings, taking 5-24. His spectacular display did not endear him to Oscar Wight. Wight was given a rare opportunity to bat, and had reached 35 in bright, confident style when Constantine called for a run, then changed his mind. A direct hit by Leo McGuirk caught Wight short of his crease, just when the substantial score that might have altered the course of his tour was looking possible. Rubbing salt into the wound, the *Newcastle Sun* reported that Wight's 'play would have been considered outstanding, were it not for the contrast with Constantine.'

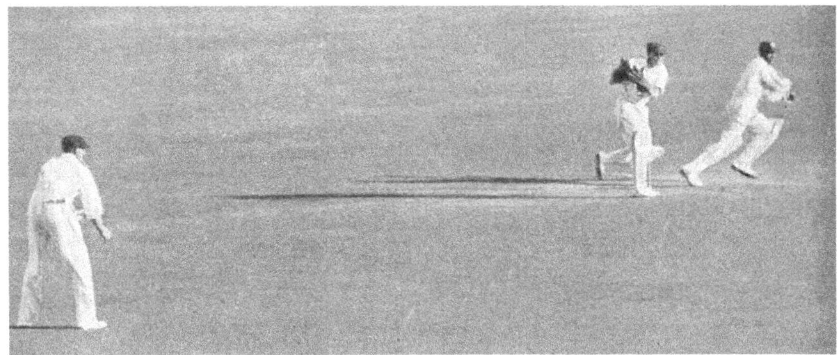

Constantine cuts a ball to the boundary (top). Hunte in the nets (above).

Australia v West Indies

Exhibition Ground, Brisbane, 16, 17, 19, 20 January 1931

Umpires: JP Orr, AE Wyeth

Australia won by an innings and 217 runs

Australia

WH Ponsford	c Birkett b Francis	109
A Jackson	lbw b Francis	0
DG Bradman	c Grant b Constantine	223
AF Kippax	b Birkett	84
SJ McCabe	c Constantine b Griffith	8
WM Woodfull	c Barrow b Griffith	17
AG Fairfax	c Sealy b Scott	9
RK Oxenham	lbw b Griffith	48
WAS Oldfield	not out	38
CV Grimmett	c Constantine b Francis	4
H Ironmonger	c Roach b Griffith	2
Extras	(2 b, 7 lb, 7 nb)	16
Total		558

Bowling

	Overs	Mdns	Runs	Wkts
Francis	26	4	76	3
Constantine	26	2	74	1
Griffith	33	4	133	4
Scott	24	1	125	1
Martin	27	3	85	0
Sealy	3	-	32	0
Birkett	7	-	16	1
Grant	1	-	1	0

West Indies

CA Roach	lbw b Oxenham	4	b McCabe	1
FR Martin	lbw b Grimmett	21	lbw b Oxenham	11
GA Headley	not out	102	c Oldfield b Ironmonger	28
JED Sealy	c McCabe b Ironmonger	3	not out	16
GC Grant	c McCabe b Grimmett	8	run out	10
LN Constantine	c Fairfax b Ironmonger	9	lbw b Oxenham	7
LS Birkett	lbw b Oxenham	8	b Grimmett	13
IM Barrow	st Oldfield b Grimmett	19	st Oldfield b Grimmett	17
OC Scott	b Oxenham	0	lbw b Grimmett	15
GN Francis	b Oxenham	8	c Oldfield b Grimmett	7
HC Griffith	lbw b Grimmett	8	c Bradman b Grimmett	12
Extras	(1 b, 2 lb)	3	(5 b, 4 lb, 2 nb)	11
Total		193		148

Bowling

	Overs	Mdns	Runs	Wkts		Overs	Mdns	Runs	Wkts
Fairfax	7	2	13	0		6	2	6	0
Oxenham	30	15	39	4		18	5	37	2
Ironmonger	26	15	43	2		15	8	29	1
Grimmett	41.3	9	95	4		14.3	4	49	5
McCabe	-	-	-	-		7	1	16	1

Ball used in the Brisbane Test.

§

The final pair of hangers was lowered from the arch of the Sydney Harbour Bridge on 23 January 1931. Dorman, Long & Co announced that steel work on the bridge would be completed early in February, by which time they would have built about 51,000 tonnes of steel into the structure. Once the steelwork on the bridge was complete, there would be no further need for the plant at Milson's Point, on the north end of the bridge, so it was to be dismantled and decommissioned – putting its 400 remaining employees out of work.

§

The strain of constant travel was beginning to wear down the West Indians. They were, mostly, men from small, lush islands, unaccustomed to long journeys through arid, dusty emptiness. 'My own island of Trinidad is only about 50 miles long,' Jack Grant told the Melbourne Herald, 'varying from 30 to 35 miles in breadth, consequently we can get from one end of it to the other in about half a day. There are about 120 miles of railway on the island. But your illimitable distances here make travel a rather formidable undertaking.' The overnight journeys were especially difficult for Frank Martin, who found that he couldn't sleep on a train. From Newcastle, the team caught a train to Sydney, then the train to Melbourne, and then they were bustled into cars for a fifty-mile drive to Geelong – and all for a minor, two-day game against Victorian Country. With Jack Grant resting, Lionel Birkett led the team for the only time. The game began fifteen minutes late, since the drive from Melbourne took longer than expected. It was dreadful preparation for a cricket match, which partly explains the debacle that followed.

The game began more or less as it was expected to do: the West Indies bowled well enough without extending themselves – Constantine sent down slow, loopy off-breaks in his first spell – and the Country team slumped to 125 for six. The only top-order batsman remaining was a diminutive 17 year-old schoolboy from Geelong College, Lindsay Hassett. The West Indians had already played against his older brother – Learie Constantine had bowled Dick Hassett first ball in the game against Victoria. But the schoolboy put up sterner resistance. He batted carefully until he reached fifty, and then produced a full array of strokes, driving and cutting with impressive timing. Late in the innings, he hit out at almost everything bowled to him scoring 56 of the 74 runs added for the last three wickets. Constantine captured the last two wickets just before stumps, but Hassett remained unbeaten, having scored 147 of his team's 327.

Weary and frustrated, the West Indies responded limply. Only two batsmen with a point to prove – Errol Hunte (50) and Frank de Caires (49) – lasted for very long. The West Indies were never in danger of defeat, but in a two-day match the follow-on margin was only 100 runs, and the Country captain, Frank Just, was delighted to enforce it. Before the West Indians turned back to Melbourne, there was time for Constantine to give the crowd the entertainment they'd come for, hammering 80 in less than an hour. But it wasn't enough to cover up the team's weakest performance of the tour.

§

Ted Theodore was reinstated as Federal Treasurer on 27 January. It had become clear that no criminal charges were to be laid against him in relation to the Mungana mine deal, and Jim Scullin announced that he 'never for one moment believed that Mr Theodore was guilty of the serious charges made against him'. Now, he thought, 'the Commonwealth Government and the country as a whole, want the services of Mr Theodore in the present difficulties… He has a very fine grip of these problems, and his inclusion in the Cabinet will be of the greatest service to the Ministry in the herculean task that faces it at this serious period of our national life.'

Not everyone was pleased with Theodore's return. Joe Lyons was furious. Partly this was because he disagreed with Theodore's expansionist approach to government spending, but mostly it was because he saw himself as the obvious candidate for the Treasury portfolio. Lyons was conservative by inclination, but had joined the Labor Party because that was what Catholics did. He promptly tendered his resignation as Minister for Works and Railways, and went to sit sat grumpily on the backbenches, contemplating his next move.

§

Dame Nellie Melba arrived in Sydney on the train from Melbourne. She was, the *Sydney Morning Herald* insisted, 'still under medical advice' but had 'left yesterday afternoon by train for the country, on a visit to relatives.' That seems to have been a piece of misdirection: in fact, Melba had entered St Vincent's Hospital. When the news of her hospitalisation spread, authorities at the hospital declined to say what her illness was, but announced that 'her condition was easier and she was resting.'

§

On 28 January, the Australian trading banks announced the new official rate of exchange: 130 Australian pounds would now be needed to buy £100 sterling.

This was a minor disaster for the West Indies Cricket Board of Control. When the Australian Board of Control agreed to provide a £3,000 guarantee against losses, the Australian pound had been at parity with sterling. Now it was worth three-quarters of the value that the West Indies Board had expected. And it was becoming increasingly clear that the West Indies Board would be calling on the guarantee at the tour's end.

§

'We lacked cohesion', was Learie Constantine's verdict. George Headley reflected that 'There was an absence of that team spirit which I should have liked very much to see.' And the embittered Oscar Wight argued that 'in the West Indies we are not afforded many opportunities for the development of a truly representative team through geographical, financial and other reasons of lesser importance but fully aware of this, we seem to develop and harbour a greater handicap – insular prejudice. We in the West Indies have yet to overcome that insular prejudice comparable to the inter-State rivalry which was such a handicap to Australian cricket some time ago. Were I able to refer to ours as rivalry, however, I should have more hope for the immediate future but I am afraid that so long as we keep our eyes closed to present conditions there is little hope of West Indies elevens ever playing as a team in the true sense of the word.'

Wight thought that it was a mistake that the assistant manager, captain, and most influential player of the side – Constantine – all came from Trinidad. He thought that a Trinidad clique had too much of a grip over the side, especially when it came to selections. There's no doubt that his perspective was jaundiced by the fact that he was relegated to such a peripheral role on the tour, but his arguments can't be dismissed out of hand, because Constantine and Headley also hinted that the touring team was not an entirely harmonious one. And the *Trinidad Sporting Chronicle* reported that Grant 'wrote to Trinidad saying that certain players had given him trouble' and 'things had not worked smoothly', although no names were named.

Constantine may not have been entirely blameless. His achievements, in cricket and off the field, have made him – quite rightly – a revered figure, but he was not burdened by false modesty. He had a justifiably high opinion of his own abilities and, during his playing days, there were some who believed that this crossed the line into conceit; he was even known to a small handful of people as 'the I specialist'. Constantine had abundant talent, self-confidence and a desire to be at the heart of the action, and that could be a difficult attitude for less gifted and secure men to handle.

The task of knitting men from different countries, backgrounds and races into a cohesive team was an extremely demanding one, especially when several members of that team were competing against each other for places in the Test side. Jack Grant had enough wit and self-awareness to understand the problem, and his work as captain was always earnest and well-intentioned. But he was a very young man who was, in many ways, a stranger to West Indies cricket. He had been asked, as Headley put it, 'to lead a team of cricketers he had never met, played with or against. In addition he lacked the experience of leading any team in a first class match and to mould this team overnight, as it were, to meet such formidable opposition, was in my opinion asking too much of him.' Grant was respected by Headley, and the rest of his team, who saw and genuinely appreciated the efforts he made, but he didn't have quite the personal standing or authority to establish a successful team culture. It probably didn't help that Joe Scheult persisted in referring to Grant as 'our little skipper'.

Grant's difficulties were compounded by the nature of the tour. There were sixteen players in the touring party, so at least five of them would be idle on any given day. It's highly demoralising to be committed to a lengthy cricket tour without playing very much cricket. Wight, Frank de Caires, Errol Hunte and Edwin St Hill received very few opportunities, and were never seriously in contention for the Test team. It's unlikely that they were very happy about this. Because Wight was a good fieldsman, he was often chosen to act as twelfth man, a task he never relished. As the tour progressed, Grant worked hard to make his side competitive, and to attract the larger crowds that might make the tour financially viable – and that meant playing his strongest team most of the time.

While players like Wight and de Caires were marginalised, Constantine – the team's leading drawcard – played in every game but one. It may be unappealing that Wight became so resentful, but it's also understandable.

There's a photograph of the West Indian team, posing in their whites and blazers on the deck of a ship. Most of the players have placed their hands neatly in their laps and settled into the blankly solemn expression usually affected on these occasions. Lionel Birkett looks ready for a funeral. But standing in the top corner, Oscar Wight is laughing uproariously, clutching the side of his head with his left hand. To his right, Frank de Caires struggles, not very successfully, to supress a giggle. And to Wight's left is grim-faced Joe Scheult, glowering with disapproval and obviously unimpressed by this breach of decorum. It's unwise to read too much into a single image, but if you're looking for a visual representation of the gulf that opened up between the two batsmen from Demerara and the team's management, this is it.

10,000 flock to Hurstville Oval on January 31 1931 to see Bradman bat for St George v Northern Districts.

7

February

Jack Lang comes up with a plan; Melba runs out of farewells; Bradman bats and bats; and Bill Ponsford has a shandy

The schedule for the West Indies tour read as though the people putting it together had struggled to get through to the end of January, and then simply gave up. The day after their game against Victorian Country, the West Indies began a three-day, first-class match against Victoria – even though Victoria was also drawn to begin its Sheffield Shield match in Brisbane on the very same day. After the game in Melbourne, the West Indians were to travel to Adelaide to play South Australia, before looping back to Melbourne for the fourth Test. It was exhausting, and deeply irrational.

§

King George V, through his private secretary, sent a telegram to the governor of New South Wales inquiring about Dame Nellie Melba's health. The governor sent 'a reassuring reply'. That was misleading.

The Melbourne *Argus* reported that Nellie Melba's condition was 'improving slowly'. It was not.

Her condition was septicaemia, a bacterial poisoning of the blood, for which there was then no known cure. In the late nineteenth century, Joseph Lister had realised that septicaemia often occurred when bacteria entered the bloodstream through the wound during surgery, and he had devised a number of precautions to reduce the risk of infection. But not every doctor followed those procedures with adequate care. Presumably, the surgeon who performed Melba's facial surgery in Paris had either used imperfectly sterilised instruments, or otherwise performed the operation under insufficiently hygienic conditions. If antibiotics had been available, there would have been some chance of attacking the infection; as it was, all that the doctors at St Vincent's could do was try to alleviate the symptoms.

They performed that task so well that Melba, forever a creature of the spotlight, felt sufficiently recovered to grant an interview to a journalist. 'There will be plenty of time to make plans when I am convalescing', she announced. 'You know, it feels quite like old times to be talking to a member of the press!'

§

With the Sheffield Shield on the line, Victoria sent its strongest team to Brisbane, even though they were to face what was virtually Queensland's third eleven. Seven of the home team would be appearing in first-class cricket for the first time, including the spinner, 'Chilla' Christ, who was drafted into the side at the last minute when Ron Oxenham came down with a temperature. At least, they would have made their debuts, if there had been any play. Instead, the Victorians were greeted with four days of incessant rain. It was, and is, common for cricket in Brisbane to be interrupted by spectacular late afternoon thunderstorms, but this was something different, the fringe of a tropical cyclone that battered the city with violent winds and a torrential, constant downpour. Not a ball was bowled; the captains never even bothered to toss. The two points they received for the washout gave Victoria an impregnable lead in the Shield competition. Queensland had dropped its best players from a match that never even started and, even if Queensland had chosen its strongest possible side, the weather would still have placed the Sheffield Shield beyond its reach.

Chilla Christ did eventually play for Queensland – seven years later. He was more fortunate than Albert Flugge, Alan Harding, Arthur Rofe and Jack Pizzey, who spent their only four days as Queensland cricketers watching rain fall. None of them was ever chosen for the State again. It was especially frustrating for Pizzey, the young slow bowler, who made a round trip of almost five hundred miles for the game, from his home in Bundaberg in the north of the State. Pizzey was a trainee schoolteacher, and had negotiated leave from the Department of Education to make the journey south. If Pizzey's cricket career was frustrated prematurely, he at least had the consolation of different successes. He became Premier of Queensland in January 1968.

§

Phar Lap rested in December and January, when the weather was hot and there were no stakes worth his trouble. The Melbourne *Globe* wrote about him anyway, engaging an anonymous expert to 'examine this latest freak animal from head to heel' and explain his success. 'Phar Lap's head', the expert opined, 'is rather small and is set upon a long neck… The muscles of the neck downward from the roots of the ears are well developed, and stand well back from the windpipe, leaving ample room for the working of the main arteries to the head. The eyes are full and intelligent looking, and show a good fighting quality.' It wasn't until the very end of this analysis that the expert hit upon 'the reason for Phar Lap's speed' – long legs.

Harry Telford's lease on the horse had run out, and instead of renewing it, he'd bought a minority share in him. He was anxious to take good care of his new asset. When the handicappers of the Sydney Cup and Newmarket Handicap asked Phar Lap to carry 10 stone 13 pounds, Telford simply scratched the horse from the field. He didn't explain why, but his reasons were clear. If racing clubs wanted Phar Lap in their meetings, he wasn't going to let them handicap him out of contention.

§

When the West Indians were playing well, Charles Macartney wrote, 'they will satisfy even the most ardent admirer of bright and breezy hitting.' This, Les Poidevin thought, was because 'a large vein of aggression runs through the batting of the side.' Poidevin informed the readers of the *Sydney Mail* that 'a characteristic of their cricket is the great pace at which, as a rule, their batsman score', which it attributed to both 'their extraordinary keenness and enthusiasm for the game' and the fact that, in the West Indies, 'the spectators watch the game in a state of excitement almost unknown elsewhere.'

Everyone seemed to agree that the West Indies played a distinctive brand of cricket – except for the West Indians. 'The idea', George Headley reflected, 'that we suffer from some sort of West Indian temperament has no meaning for me.' There was no real similarity between the way Frank Martin and Jack Grant played – carefully, defensively – and the English-inflected off-side strokeplay of Frank de Caires or the dazzling improvisations produced by Constantine. Headley's own technique was different again – fundamentally orthodox, but embellished with a couple of distinctive touches, like his ability to drive a half-volley high over mid-off from the back foot.

The expectation that the West Indians would be cavalier entertainers was partly created by Constantine, who embodied that approach. It was also informed by an underlying racism – there was an expectation that black West Indians would play flamboyant and unorthodox cricket, which was thrilling but also undisciplined. Australian journalists often pointed out that Grant, de Caires and Wight 'had the benefit of English coaching', as if there were a certain kind of skill and wisdom that could be imparted only in that way. The truth was rather more complicated. No one knew Constantine better than CLR James, who saw how the all-rounder devoted 'hours of hard labour' to developing his skills. 'No cricketer', James wrote, 'has worked at his cricket and studied it more than this so original and creative of cricketers. So much for the persistent illusion of West Indian spontaneity.'

§

In power, but without power to change much that mattered, Prime Minister Jim Scullin convened a conference of State Premiers in Canberra to seek agreement on a plan to tackle the Depression. The Labor Party controlled the Federal government, as well as the governments of New South Wales, Victoria and South Australia, which should have enabled it to shape the agenda of the conference. Instead, it tore itself apart.

The opening of the conference did nothing to inspire confidence: Scullin openly admitted 'the seriousness of the outlook', before confessing that he 'had no concrete suggestions to put forward'. That, he proposed, was the duty of the conference. Scullin's reticence created a policy vacuum that Jack Lang was eager to fill. He put forward a radical plan of his own. Government budgets, he argued, were weighed down by the need to pay interest to British lenders. In New South Wales, the annual interest commitment was £8 million, 'a burden which Australia has no right to carry. Most of the debt was incurred during the war years and because of the war. Money was borrowed at inflated prices and must now be repaid during a period of deflation. Where two shiploads of wool or wheat were required to pay a portion of our interest a few years ago, four shipments are now required to pay the same amount. The effect of such manipulation is that Australia's debts and interest payments have been doubled.'

The solution, Lang insisted, was for Australian governments to stop paying interest to British bondholders until they agreed to a temporary moratorium on interest payments for the duration of the Depression – of the kind which Britain was then negotiating for itself with the United States. The choice, he maintained, was 'whether hundreds of Australians are to go without the necessaries of life so that the international money ring shall have its pound of flesh, or whether the British investor shall have repaid to him an amount equal in fact to the amount he lent.'

'Repudiation' was the central plank in Lang's plan, which also included a reduction in government interest rates and a departure from the gold standard (which required currency issued by the government to be backed by a holding of gold). It isn't entirely clear whether Lang genuinely believed that this was a viable solution to the crisis, and Ted Theodore was quick to point out its obvious flaw – if Australia repudiated its existing debt, it would have no hope of ever raising the new debt it still needed. But the Lang Plan was, at heart, a political calculation rather than an economic one. It enabled Lang to project himself as a strong, bold leader, who was unafraid to stand up for the interests of ordinary people against the rapacity of British bankers. In a series of public speeches promoting his plan, he pointed out that Britain had suspended the payment of war reparations by Germany, yet continued to demand payment from its ally, Australia. Opponents of his plan, he insisted, were concerned only for 'England and the oversea financial interests. It is their task to belittle the country in which they live, to repudiate soldiers' pensions, take away old age pensions, to withdraw social services such as hospital facilities, to belittle Australia's national effort in the war.'

Scullin and the other Premiers rejected the Lang Plan, but the New South Wales Labor Party endorsed it. After Eddie Ward won a by-election for the Federal seat of East Sydney, campaigning on the Lang Plan, Scullin refused to allow him to sit with the Labor Party caucus, because he had not been elected on Labor policies. Ward promptly formed a splinter group within the Federal Parliament, together with three other Lang supporters, who soon became known as Lang Labor. The fragmentation of the party had begun.

§

On the first weekend of February, Don Bradman hit an unbeaten half-century to help his club St George, defeat High Chilvers' Northern District. Ten thousand people crammed into Hurstville Oval to watch him bat. Grade cricket matches remained attractive for spectators even as attendance at first-class games declined, because spectators could walk to their local ground (saving the cost of a train or tram fare) and paid only a few pennies for entrance. The Gordon club's medium-pacer, Jim Sullivan, enjoyed playing in front of the huge crowds that Bradman drew to suburban games, but he was under no illusion as to why they were there: 'Well, they'd come to see you get slaughtered.'

§

The Australian agents for Berger's Paints proudly announced that their product had been selected for the painting of the Sydney Harbour Bridge. Three coats would be applied, each using about 20,000 gallons of paint. In total, about 600 tons of paint was needed to complete the job – although the job would never really be completed, since the corrosive effect of the sea air meant that the bridge required more or less constant repainting.

Painting the Harbour Bridge meant something different to the Sydney artist, Grace Cossington Smith. Her vivid modernist work, The Bridge in Curve, had been rejected by the Society of Artists, but was shown during the summer of 1930-31 in the Macquarie Galleries' annual 'Contemporaries' exhibition. Her work was derided by the art critic for *The Bulletin*, who was predisposed to ridicule anything new, and called her work 'artless', sneering that 'deliberately crude draughtsmanship and monotonously careless brush strokes may be justified if they produce a definite and aimed-at effect, but they become a wearisome affectation if they don't.' Although the *Sydney Morning Herald* mistakenly described The Bridge in Curve as an 'oil painting' (it was, in fact, tempera on cardboard – who, in a Depression, could afford oils and canvas?), its critic otherwise grasped the point of it, finding it to be 'a remarkable composition of crowded detail and abrupt colours, with the massive ironwork (before the arch was joined) towering over everything, and thrown into bold relief against a peculiar luminous glow.' That luminosity gives the painting an extraordinary energy, as the opposite ends of the arch seem to surge towards each other like two colossal mechanical beasts, while the fact that the source of the light appears to be a sunrise presents the bridge as an almost religious symbol of hope and renewal. Cossington Smith produced several studies of the bridge while it was being built, only to lose all interest in it once it was complete. The finished object was a disappointingly static agglomeration of steel and stone, with none of the dynamism of the construction project.

§

Presented with a second-string Victorian attack and a slow Melbourne pitch, the West Indians cashed in. Clifford Roach and George Headley hit rapid centuries, Jack Grant hit 84, and Frank Martin, Derek Sealy and Ivan Barrow all spent valuable time at the crease. But no-one enjoyed the occasion more than Frank de Caires. Going into the game, de Caires had scored only five first-class runs in more than ten weeks in Australia: now he showed why it was that he had been selected in the first place. In the first innings, he opened up after a slow start, driving the ball past cover with tremendous power, and reaching 76. He followed that with a lively 64 in his second effort, made in only 71 minutes, and including a huge six, driven over mid-off. The attack was modest, but suddenly de Caires looked like an international cricketer again.

He even took a wicket. Since leaving school, de Caires had very rarely bowled in any class of cricket, but the final day of the game was extremely hot, and Grant decided to give a break to his regular bowlers – who did not include Constantine, who was rested for the only time on the tour. So George Headley sent down four overs of leg spin, and de Caires, who 'tossed up slow deliveries', bowled four overs of whatever it was that he bowled. It worked, too, with wicket-keeper Stan Quin blasting a drive straight to wide mid-on.

The catcher was Oscar Wight, fielding as substitute, and quietly brooding. After the tour, he complained of 'seeing some tried who would not try, and others who would have tried still waiting for a trial.' No doubt Wight did the best he could with the meagre opportunities he was offered, but the Victorian match did not lighten his mood. After Grant set Victoria more than 400 to win in four hours, the ninth wicket fell at 250, with twenty minutes to play. Victoria's last batsman, Edwin Healy, promptly edged a straightforward chance to third slip, where it was spilled – by Oscar Wight. Victoria escaped with a draw.

§

Wight might have been given a game against South Australia in Adelaide, but Edward Bartlett had recovered from his broken finger, and Jack Grant was anxious to see whether he could regain his form. And Frank de Caires had earned another opportunity to stake his claim for Test selection, so yet again Wight sat in the dressing room and looked on.

Jack Grant often said that the West Indians had come to Australia to learn, and the lesson they were taught in Adelaide was on the importance of maintaining pressure. They looked like winning for the entire match, right up to the point when they lost. Grant set the tone himself, contributing his only century of the tour – which included, to his lasting satisfaction, a six from Grimmett's bowling that landed in the grandstand. Headley made a sedate half-century, Constantine a rapid one, and although Grimmett captured five wickets, they were expensive, costing him 144 runs. Constantine than ran through the South Australian batting until the home side's fifth wicket fell with the score on 46. Philip Lee led a lower-order recovery, but even so the West Indies led by 105 runs on the first innings.

When the West Indies batted again, they tried to force the pace to allow time for a result, and were dismissed more cheaply than they should have been. Even so, the South Australians needed 314 to win, which seemed unlikely when the first four wickets fell for 105 runs. But the West Indians were a bowler down, and the bowler was Constantine, who complained of a sprain. Tommy Scott bowled beautifully, though, and when the ninth wicket fell, the home side still needed 22 runs. The batsmen handled the pressure better than the fielding side and the score mounted slowly; in the excitement, Errol Hunte allowed a ball from Frank Martin to slip away down the leg side for three byes. Charlie Walker then edged Martin past his leg stump, and the ball ran away for three more runs. The batsmen then needed three to win, and Walker lobbed a ball from Scott tamely into the on-side, running a single as it fell harmlessly between three converging fieldsmen. Tom Carlton settled the game on the next delivery, popping the ball just out of reach of Griffith at short leg, and scampering back for the second run.

It was a difficult game for Errol Hunte, who made little impression with the bat, and conceded 31 byes altogether. That performance probably ended whatever chance he had of regaining his Test place, while Frank de Caires, who was dismissed twice by Grimmett, also failed to grasp his opportunity. In the first innings, he attacked, hitting two beautiful drives for four, but was stumped for only 14. Concentrating on defence in his second innings, he was caught behind, blocking, for six. Edwin St Hill was uncharacteristically expensive in the second innings, leaking 85 runs from 17 overs. None of these three men ever played in another Test.

§

Returning to Melbourne, the West Indians entertained an unusual visitor at their hotel – Sam Morris, who had played for Victoria for eleven years and made a single Test appearance for Australia in 1884-85. Morris is sometimes referred to as the first West Indian to play Test cricket, but in fact he was born in Hobart in 1855, and it was his father (who came from Barbados) and maternal grandparents who were West Indian. Learie Constantine remembered him as 'a black Barbadian… who had come to Australia gold-hunting fifty years earlier', which was not quite right – although Morris' family had moved from Tasmania to Victoria to join the goldfields not long after his birth. By the time he met the West Indians, Morris had been blind for more than twenty years, but he spent several happy hours with the team, and Constantine described his visit as his 'most interesting memory' of his time in Melbourne.

§

The Melbourne Test was a competitive contest for about an hour, which was the time it took for the West Indies to reach 50 for one. Here's Learie Constantine's description of the game, in full: 'we lost the fourth Test'. George Headley, only slightly more expansive, called it 'another catastrophe for us'. After the West Indies made a solid start, the game turned as quickly as the Melbourne weather. When play began, it was stiflingly hot and dusty; by the afternoon, it was raining, and play was ended early for bad light. By that time, Australia, with nine wickets standing, already had a lead of 98.

Most of the damage was done by Bert Ironmonger, who knew precisely how to exploit his home pitch. Ironmonger bowled a touch faster than most spinners, and seldom gave the ball much air, so it was difficult for the batsmen to use their feet to attack him; but he also bowled slowly enough to extract uncommonly sharp turn for a finger spinner. A faster straight ball often earned him lbw decisions, and when the ball was new, he could swerve it in towards the right-handers. He did all this with relentless, almost mechanical, accuracy. Frank Martin, who had batted soundly, missed the faster straight ball. Lionel Birkett got one that turned away, and edged it to McCabe at slip. George Headley misjudged a drive, and picked out Archie Jackson at deep mid-on. Grant, as usual, defended stoutly until Ironmonger found his outside edge, and Oldfield made no mistake behind the stumps. Edward Bartlett leaned forward to defend, was beaten by the spin, and was stumped; the very next ball, Ivan Barrow leaned forward to defend, was beaten by the spin, and nicked a catch to McCabe at slip. The innings ended when Herman Griffith fended a soft catch to slip, giving Ironmonger his seventh wicket. In just over an hour, the West Indies had lost nine wickets for 48 runs.

Australia's reply was ruthless, and the West Indians were hopelessly outplayed. Even the one wicket they took on the opening day came from a mistake: Constantine beat Ponsford's outside edge and Barrow, standing up to the stumps, missed the ball completely – only to be credited with the stumping when the ball rebounded from his pads and dislodged the bails. The decision surprised Ponsford, who paused to point out that Barrow hadn't taken the ball, but there was no reprieve from the umpire. Bradman gave Woodfull a start of 49 minutes, but soon caught up to his score, needing only 45 minutes to reach fifty. He was unbeaten on 92 at stumps, and the Australians appeared set for a massive total.

The complexion of the game was changed by overnight rain, and the pitch was soft when play resumed. The West Indian bowlers received just enough encouragement to fight their way back into the game. They were helped by some poor running between the wickets by the Australians. Bradman was rapped on the pad by Constantine, and looked at the umpire (who refused the appeal) rather than his partner, Woodfull, who had taken off for a leg-bye and had no chance of regaining his crease. Then Bradman had a complete misunderstanding with Stan McCabe, as a result of which both batsmen finished up at the same end. Bradman walked from the field, only to be recalled by the umpires, who somehow ruled that McCabe was the man dismissed. Bradman was struck twice on the body by Herman Griffith, but carried his score past 150 before he mistimed a drive at Martin and was well caught by Clifford Roach.

Archie Jackson batted when the pitch was at its worst. He was, one reporter thought, 'sound and stylish', if a little more subdued than usual. He had batted for almost an hour and barely made a false stroke when Constantine enticed him into playing at a ball outside off stump, which he edged to Birkett in the slips. No one at the ground imagined that they were watching his final innings in a first-class match.

Constantine, Martin and Griffith all bowled well, but Bill Woodfull was able to declare when the pitch was still tricky for batting. The game was all over on the second day. This time, Alan Fairfax enjoyed the rare opportunity to bowl in helpful conditions, made the ball kick unpredictably, and collected the best bowling figures of his Test career. Tommy Scott top-scored for the West Indians, and had the satisfaction of slogging Grimmett for six with his last scoring stroke in Test cricket.

The result – defeat by an innings and plenty – was bad enough, but the game was a financial disaster, too. The financial health of the tour depended upon four or five big gates in Melbourne, but on the first day, only 3,969 people turned up – half the number who had attended the first day of the match against Victoria's second-string side. They paid just over £210. On the second day, 9,030 people paid £470. It was a tiny fraction of what was needed to balance the books. By now, the West Indies tour faced precisely the same problem as the Australian government – how to deal with its debt. One newspaper reported that, with two matches remaining in the tour, the West Indians still needed £4500 to break even.

Presentation cricket match ball given to Bert Ironmonger for taking 7 wickets for 23 against the West Indies on 13 February 1931. Australian Sports Museum.

Australia v West Indies

Melbourne Cricket Ground, 13, 14 February 1931

Umpires: AN Barlow, J Richards

Australia won by an innings and 122 runs

West Indies

CA Roach	c Kippax b Grimmett	20	lbw b Fairfax	7
FR Martin	lbw b Ironmonger	17	c Oldfield b Fairfax	10
GA Headley	c Jackson b Ironmonger	33	c Fairfax b Ironmonger	11
LS Birkett	c McCabe b Ironmonger	0	c Jackson b Ironmonger	13
EL Bartlett	st Oldfield b Ironmonger	9	b Fairfax	6
GC Grant	c Oldfield b Ironmonger	0	c McCabe b Ironmonger	3
LN Constantine	c Jackson b Grimmett	7	c Kippax b Fairfax	10
IM Barrow	c Fairfax b Ironmonger	0	c Oxenham b Ironmonger	13
OC Scott	run out	11	not out	20
GN Francis	not out	0	c Jackson b Grimmett	0
HC Griffith	c Fairfax b Ironmonger	0	b Grimmett	4
Extras	(2 nb)	2	(3 b, 6 lb, 1 nb)	10
Total		99		107

Bowling

	Overs	Mdns	Runs	Wkts		Overs	Mdns	Runs	Wkts
Fairfax	5	-	14	0		14	2	31	4
Oxenham	6	1	14	0		-	-	-	-
Ironmonger	20	7	23	7		17	4	56	4
Grimmett	19	7	46	2		4.4	-	10	2

Australia

WM Woodfull	run out	83
WH Ponsford	st Barrow b Constantine	24
DG Bradman	c Roach b Martin	152
A Jackson	c Birkett b Constantine	15
SJ McCabe	run out	2
AG Fairfax	c Birkett b Martin	16
AF Kippax	b Martin	24
RK Oxenham	c Constantine b Griffith	0
WAS Oldfield	not out	1
CV Grimmett		
H Ironmonger		
Extras	(7 b, 3 lb, 1 nb)	11
Total	(8 declared)	328

Bowling

	Overs	Mdns	Runs	Wkts
Francis	13	-	51	0
Griffith	8	1	33	1
Scott	11	-	47	0
Constantine	25	4	83	2
Martin	30.2	3	91	3
Birkett	2	-	12	0

Archie Jackson pulled out of the New South Wales team to play the West Indies in Sydney. He was feeling very, very tired. He put it down to a year of nonstop cricket, and the lingering effects of influenza.

§

While the West Indian batsmen struggled against Ironmonger and Grimmett in the fourth Test, the most destructive player of spin in the Caribbean was engaged in an entirely different international sporting contest. Jamaica hosted a visit from the Czechoslovakian amateur football team, which was on its way to South America to play in Uruguay. Czechoslovakia had little trouble winning the only international match ever played between the two countries, and the score might have become embarrassing but for an exceptional performance by the Jamaican goalkeeper, Clarence Passailaigue.

§

His work behind the stumps never gave the impression that Ivan Barrow was a natural wicket-keeper. He worked hard, applied himself diligently, and continued to make costly mistakes at important moments. The contrast between Barrow and Australia's smooth, predatory Bert Oldfield was almost painful. Curiously, Jack Grant never lost faith in Barrow, possibly because he always made an obvious effort, and perhaps because he could be relied upon not to surrender his wicket lightly (even though he rarely made a substantial score). It was also relatively common at the time for wicket-keepers to be assessed by the number of byes they allowed, and on that measure, Barrow performed surprisingly well, partly because he stood back more than most other keepers. In his report to the Board of Control at the end of the tour, Grant went so far out of his way to praise Barrow's work behind the stumps that it seemed almost as if he was trying to persuade himself.

The *Kingston Gleaner* thought there was another reason why Errol Hunte was never given a chance in the Tests. In the match against Queensland, it reported, Hunte 'with great show and confidence appealed for a catch off V Goodwin... behind the wicket and on the umpire negativing the appeal Hunte proceeded to make a demonstration in seeming disgust of the decision, throwing down the ball with a certain amount of rage at the same time.' This episode, curiously, was not mentioned at all in the Australian press, but certainly would not have impressed Grant, if in fact it occurred.

It wasn't only Grant with whom Barrow was popular. A journalist from the *Herald* met with him as he was 'in the act of opening a letter from a girl who wanted his autograph. "I don't know her", he said, "She says here, 'you might remember me, I was wearing a light straw hat with flowers round the brim.' Hmm. There's such a lot of light straw hats about just now!"'

§

Phar Lap returned to the track on 16 February, at the Victorian Amateur Turf Club's autumn meeting at Caulfield. The St George Stakes, run over nine furlongs, carried a purse of just £750, and only three horses were prepared to challenge Phar Lap for it. It was a weight-for-age event, and Phar Lap wasn't remotely bothered by carrying 9 stone 7 pounds. Jim Pike allowed Black Duchess to lead the field into the straight, and then let Phar Lap romp home by two and a half lengths.

It was Phar Lap's eleventh win in succession, and carried his earnings to £47,462, only £835 behind the Australian record-holder, Amounis.

§

'A batsman in my opinion has to adapt himself', was George Headley's conclusion. 'Our batsmen could not. A test batsman must be able to play on all sorts of wickets.' He didn't name names, but he might have been thinking about Clifford Roach. After Headley, Roach was the team's finest batsman, but his returns on tour were disappointing. He usually looked good; he usually began well; but he seldom made all that many runs. 'Roach can bat', wrote the journalist 'Johnny' Moyes early in the tour. 'His footwork is delightful, he clips the ball hard; and finds the gaps. He loses nothing in comparison with recent English visitors either in style or execution.' He was one of the few West Indian players who used his feet to attack the spinners successfully. But he couldn't turn promising starts into tall scores. Partly this was due to a flaw in his technique: his defensive bat wasn't always straight, so he developed a habit of chopping balls from the medium-pacers – Hurwood, Fairfax, McCabe – onto his stumps. Sometimes, his desire to attack the spinners resulted in a loose stroke that cost him his wicket. And sometimes he was plain unlucky. In the Melbourne Test, according to The *Sun*, Jack Grant 'played a ball straight to Hurwood at slip and ran. Roach came through and, although, from the Press stand, he seemed to have safely grounded his bat as Oldfield whipped off the balls, Umpire Borwick said 'Out', apparently much to the surprise of West Indies player.'

This wasn't the only time the umpires surprised the West Indians. They had been particularly upset by an incident in the Sydney Test, when they believed that Alan Kippax had been dismissed by George Francis, who held a brilliant, juggling catch, from his own bowling, only for umpire George Borwick to rule that the ball had somewhere touched the ground. 'We suffered badly from the umpiring during that tour', Constantine complained. 'I do not think this is an unfair comment. Our appeals against the light were disregarded, but once or twice when things were running our way on a wet wicket, play ended rather suddenly before time. There were some queer decisions about catches; when we got them something was wrong with them, but it was not so the other way round.'

It was commonplace for visiting teams, especially losing visiting teams, to grumble about their hosts' umpires. But Constantine's complaints probably had some substance. Certainly the standard of umpiring was variable, because instead of appointing the most proficient umpires for each Test, the Australian Board of Control, as an economy, decided that local umpires would be appointed by the host Association in each city. They were, quite literally, hometown umpires. They may not have been biased, but nor were they the best available. George Hele and Arthur Jenkins stood in Adelaide, George Borwick, Henry Armstrong and Wally French in Sydney, James Orr and Arthur Wyeth in Brisbane, and Andy Barlow and Joseph Richards in Melbourne. The matches against the West Indies were the only Tests in which Jenkins, French, Orr, Wyeth, Armstrong and Richards ever umpired. Things were no better in the State matches: the first game in Melbourne was officiated by Bert Nichols, the sixth-best umpire in Victoria, who was never appointed to a Sheffield Shield match. Nichols cherished the occasion so much that he collected the autographs of the West Indian players at the end of the first day's play.

After two Tests, Jack Grant wrote to the Australian Board of Control asking that the best available umpires be appointed in the remaining matches, but that was just one more unsuccessful appeal.

§

In London, in Parliament, Lady Astor explained England's recent defeat in the Ashes series. American by birth, and wealthy – twice – by marriage, Nancy Astor had become, in 1919, the first woman to take a seat in the House of Commons. She was a Conservative, a dedicated Christian Scientist, and a ferocious opponent of alcohol, which she suspected of somehow causing her son's homosexuality. During a debate on the Liquor Traffic Bill, she complained that restrictions on the sale of alcohol were being unreasonably obstructed by the House of Lords, whose members should be referred to as having, not a peerage, but a beerage. 'Why we were beaten at cricket?' she thundered, 'It was because the Australian players did not drink!'

Ten members of the English team, then touring South Africa, sent a response to the *Daily Express*, which read 'We thank Lady Astor for the great interest she takes in Test cricket, but beg to state that she is guilty of a terminological inexactitude. For further information we suggest that she applies to Richardson, Kippax, Ponsford, Grimmett, Oldfield or Hornibrook.' Lady Astor didn't make those enquiries, but the Australian press did. Alan Kippax grinned that he 'had no opinion to offer', while the obliging Bert Oldfield confessed that 'I would not say that the Australians were any more teetotal than their English opponents. At the various functions at which members of both teams attended, I drank a glass of wine with the Englishmen, but I drank more cups of tea with the same men.' Bill Ponsford primly refused to enter into the joke, taking offence at being named in the English team's telegram and announcing that 'I am practically a teetotaller, my last drink being a shandy on New Year's Eve.'

§

On 18 February, the New South Wales Minister for Works, Mark Davidson, met engineer John Bradfield and Lawrence Ennis of Dorman Long at the southern end of the Sydney Harbour Bridge, and together they walked across to Milson's Point, becoming the first people to complete a crossing on the bridge's decking – even though the work was 'not quite finished'.

On their return to Sydney, the West Indian cricketers were invited to inspect the bridge, and were taken on a walk along the decking. They came to a point, Jack Grant recalled, where the footpath gave way to 'a six-feet gap which could only be crossed by a single plank. Some of our players refused to make the crossing, and I had every sympathy with them, for the water below seemed far away. Moreover, it seemed to have some magnetic attraction. Yet I took the risk and crossed over and back, alive to tell the tale.'

§

Don Bradman's unprecedented success sparked a lively debate over the question of whether he was a greater batsman than Victor Trumper. Jack Worrall, who had played for Australia alongside Trumper, announced that 'it would appear, although it almost sounds like sacrilege, that a greater batsman than either Victor Trumper has arrived.' Arthur Mailey, who idolised Trumper, sat on the fence, equivocating that Trumper was a great batsman and Bradman a great rungetter. Hunter Hendry marginally favoured Trumper over Bradman, mostly because modern 'bowling is very mediocre', although he admitted that 'I never really saw Trumper at his best.' A strikingly similar discussion compared the merits of Phar Lap and Carbine, winner of the 1890 Melbourne Cup. Did Bradman make more runs than Trumper? Maybe so, but look at the inferior pitches Trumper had to play on. Was Phar Lap faster than Carbine? Probably, but the tracks are faster now. Had Phar Lap won more money? Yes, but that's inflation. Look at the bowlers Trumper had to contend with; consider the fields Carbine beat. These debates rattled on, never capable of reaching any sensible conclusion. It helped to sell newspapers.

§

For many Australians, beer had become an unaffordable luxury. Some publicans tried to stay in business by slashing their prices – there were places where the price of a pint fell from ninepence to fivepence – but that didn't prevent an unprecedented boom in home brewing. Newspapers published dozens of recipes for beer substitutes: honey beer, treacle beer, dandelion beer – anything affordable that could be used to add flavour to water before being fermented with yeast in a laundry tub. Home brewing became so popular that the Minister for Customs, Frank Forde, issued a stern warning that 'the

WEST INDIES TEAM

From left to right the names are:—
Top Row.—Mr. R. H. Mallett (manager), E. St. Hill, F. I. de Caires, O. C. Scott, H. C. Griffith, G. Francis, L. N. Constantine, Mr. J. E. Scheult (assistant manager).
Centre Row.—G. Headley, O. S. Wight, L. S. Birkett (vice-captain), G. C. Grant (captain), F. R. Martin, C. A. Roach.
Front Row.—E. L. Bartlett, E. A. C. Hunte, J. E. Sealy, and I. Barrow.

George Headley in the Sydney nets.

making of any beer containing more than two percent of spirit by any unlicensed person is illegal.' He emphasised than 'any beer brewed from standard recipes' was likely to contain more than two percent alcohol, and that 'offenders will be prosecuted'.

§

By the time the West Indians returned to Sydney, it was clear that their tour was not going to break even, so Joe Scheult engaged in earnest discussions with Charles Bull, treasurer to the Australian Board of Control, to consider where economies might be found. It was agreed that the team would no longer catch taxis from their hotel to practice or matches, but would take the tram instead. One player told a journalist that this was no hardship, because it allowed the team to see more of Sydney and meet more of its people.

The two treasurers also agreed to try to attract a larger crowd by reducing the charges for admission. Grandstand admission for the final Test was set at three shillings, and the outer ground charge was one shilling and sixpence. Even those charges were way beyond the reach of too many people. Only a couple of years earlier, a day at the cricket had been cheap entertainment. Now, it felt like an extravagant indulgence.

§

New South Wales wasn't quite at full strength for its second game against the West Indies; apart from Jackson, Bert Oldfield and Alan Fairfax were unavailable. The State selectors decided it was a good opportunity to have a look at Albert Bennett, a bricklayer from Port Kembla, who was enjoying a spectacular season in the Illawarra district, and had scored 95 against the tourists for New South Wales Country.

The Sydney pitch was fast, and Clifford Roach and George Headley enjoyed the feeling of the ball coming on to the bat. No one made a very big score, but Roach, Headley, Grant, Sealy and Constantine all played attractively. Constantine lashed a six and six fours, one of which injured Jack Fingleton, who collided with the fence while chasing the ball, and needed to leave the field. Dr Archie Blue, a vice-president of the New South Wales Cricket Association who had once tossed up left arm spin for Sydney University, took a break from watching the game to stitch up the wound.

Derek Sealy, who timed his drives beautifully, charmed the Sydney crowd, but not Oscar Wight. Wight went in to bat shortly before tea, and played carefully against Hugh Chilvers until the interval. Almost as soon as play resumed, Sealy punched a drive straight to Stan McCabe at cover, and ran. McCabe's pick up was sure, his return pinpoint-accurate, and Wight's tour descended further into misery.

The New South Wales openers – Wendell Bill and wicket-keeper Hugh Davidson, standing in for his injured Waverley clubmate Fingleton – had made a cautious start, adding 36 runs, when Constantine entered the attack. 'I had been watching the way they shaped to the going-away ball', he remembered, 'and I laid my plans accordingly. Davidson was facing me and I let him have a very fast off-break. He shaped at it just as he had done to the outswingers, and his wicket fell in a heap to my first ball. But that only brought Don Bradman in his place, which was doubtful consolation! No use giving Bradman the same – Bradman notices everything that happens. So, instead, I swung the ball from the leg side. Bradman played rather an unusual stroke to that, steering the ball away through the slips. A very pretty stroke indeed, and I decided to "feed" it, to calm him down.' After a few overs of outswing, Bradman had reached ten, and then 'I bowl him a "Davidson's Ruin", but rather slower, so as to bring Don out to make that pet stroke as usual; he does so before realising that there is a devil in it; and his off stump goes for a walk. Don gives me a sour grin and walks back to the pavilion.'

Not long afterwards, Stan McCabe chopped another of Constantine's fast off-cutters into his stumps. New South Wales were dismissed for only 190, with Constantine claiming six wickets in only 9.3 overs. The West Indies, playing with the kind of ruthless touch that had eluded them throughout their tour, seized the advantage, piling up 403 runs in just over five hours as the pitch eased. Derek Sealy won back his Test place with a stylish 92; Constantine hit explosively for 93, and Tommy Scott flogged the tired bowling for an unbeaten 67.

Grant's declaration set New South Wales a target of 553 in a day and a half. Bradman, as always, was the key, and he hurried to 73 in only 78 minutes. Then a ball from Herman Griffith skidded through a touch low, and Bradman was trapped in front. Yet New South Wales had no thought of playing for a draw; instead, Alan Kippax and Stan McCabe hammered the bowling, piling on 174 runs in a little more than two hours. At 314 for three, it seemed almost possible that the home side could pull off its improbable chase. But Frank Martin made the breakthrough, accounting for McCabe, and George Francis settled the issue with some, fast, straight, uncomplicated bowling. The West Indies won by 86 runs. It was a perfect preparation for the final Test.

§

St Vincent's Hospital took to issuing opaque daily reports on Nellie Melba's condition, and journalists scanned them in search of meaning. 'She spent a comfortable night', was a typically unhelpful formulation. 'Slightly better' led to the headline 'Melba on the mend'. 'Slightly worse' prompted 'Melba condition still serious'.

By mid-February it became impossible to avoid the truth. Melba's family gathered at the hospital, and her friends revealed that she was weak, had a high temperature, spent most of the day asleep and found it difficult to speak. She attributed her disease, it was said, to 'a germ caught in Cairo' a year earlier. On the afternoon of Sunday 22 February, St Vincent's Hospital announced that her condition was critical, and she died, surrounded by her family, the next afternoon.

§

Here's how Learie Constantine described Albert Bennett's first innings in first-class cricket: 'Griffith gets somebody for 0.'

And not only for 0, but bowled, first ball, for 0. Bennett's second effort was little better, though he hit a couple of clean drives down the ground before Tommy Scott removed him for 16. He didn't take a wicket. And the game changed his life.

During the breaks in play, Bennett spent time talking with Constantine, and he revealed that he had been born at St Helen's, in Lancashire, before moving to Australia with his family when he was ten years old. Constantine told him that St Helen's had a cricket team, and that they might be interested in a man who had played for New South Wales. What was more, Bennett was qualified by birth to play for Lancashire, so the county club might be interested in him, too.

The upshot was that, two months later, Albert Bennett sailed to England to try his luck with St Helen's Recreational. But he never appeared for the club – Lancashire got there first, signing him to the county staff in mid-

June, within a couple of weeks of his arrival in England, mostly on the strength of his leg-spin bowling. Bennett's timing was good: Lancashire was in the process of parting company with its long-serving leg-spinner, Dick Tyldesley, and there was an opportunity for a new slow bowler. Bennett was disqualified (by opaque rules and his one appearance for New South Wales) from appearing in the County Championship for twelve months from the date of his signing, so he bowled at the members, worked on the ground, and played second eleven games until June 1932, when he was selected for his debut against Glamorgan at Blackburn. No sooner had the captains tossed, than Bennett began to display symptoms of influenza, and he was sent home, becoming possibly the only player not to see even a single ball bowled in his first county match (in fact he missed little, as rain prevented any play after the first day). His career ended in failure, as most careers do, but for a time in 1933, he carved out a niche in the Lancashire side, contributing useful runs low in the order, and collecting valuable wickets. He scored a fifty against Glamorgan; against Leicestershire, he scored 47 and took 4-49, bowling his county to victory. He was released by Lancashire at the end of the 1935 season, and returned to Australia, but he'd enjoyed four years as a professional cricketer, and all because of a conversation with Learie Constantine.

§

The big event of the VATC autumn race meeting was the Futurity Stakes, which paid £2,500 to the winner and attracted a field of eleven. Phar Lap, despite a handicap of 10 stone 3 pounds, was the 2 to 1 favourite, ahead of a highly fancied contender called Waterline. The stewards had trouble getting the horses into the starting gates, and somehow, when the barrier lifted, Phar Lap missed the start. For the first half of the race, Phar Lap sat at the very back of the field, and Jim Pike was obliged to take the horse out wide to many any headway, while Mystic Peak made a tremendous run along the rail. There was a moment when Mystic Peak looked a certain winner, but Phar Lap finished powerfully, and surged home to win by a neck.

The victory made Phar Lap the first horse to win stakes of more than £50,000 in Australia.

§

It was difficult to assess Learie Constantine's performances on the tour. He was easily the leading wicket-taker in the team, by far the best fieldsman, and he was the most successful batsman other than Headley. In every State match he had done something spectacular. He was the single greatest attraction in the team, a phenomenal entertainer. And yet his record in the Test matches was dismal.

Unlike Headley, Constantine had been unable to adapt his game to the conditions and the stronger opposition he found in Australia. This wasn't a failure of intelligence: Constantine was a deeply thoughtful cricketer. And his lack of success with the ball was due, at least partly, to Australia's formidable batting strength and the fallible catching of his team-mates. Mostly, though, it was due to his refusal to compromise. If the pitches were too slow for fast bowlers, he tried to prove that he could bowl fast anyway. If the Australian bowling was too accurate to allow him to hit successfully, he hit anyway. He had no desire to play attritional cricket – he wanted to succeed on his own terms, forcing the Australians to play his way, rather than bending to the way they played. It was, in its way, an impressive act of defiance and self-belief. But it hadn't worked, and now he had only one game left to prove that he could still be a match-winner when the match was a Test in Australia.

§

The final game of the tour began at the Sydney Cricket Ground on 27 February. The reduced entry charges didn't produce the large crowd that Joe Scheult had hoped for: only 7518 people attended on the first day. Derek Sealey replaced Lionel Birkett in the West Indies team, the vice-captain's form having fallen away badly since his promising start to the series at Adelaide.

Jack Grant won the toss, and sent Clifford Roach and Frank Martin out to open the batting. In Alan Fairfax's first over, Martin punched a short delivery away past point, and the batsman ran up and down, realising as they completed three runs that the pitch was flat and fast, the ball was coming nicely on to the bat, and the outfield offered them full value for their strokes. In Fairfax's next over, Roach glanced a ball on leg stump that raced to the fence for four more runs, and then he drove Oxenham past mid-off for another boundary. There could be no excuses if the West Indians failed today.

Ironmonger joined the attack when 29 runs had been scored, but although he was as accurate as ever, the pitch gave him no assistance, and Roach and Martin played him defensively but easily. Then Grimmett took the ball, and Martin surprised everyone by using his feet to reach the pitch of the ball, and twice driving the spinner to the off-side fence. It took only 56 minutes for the openers to carry the total past fifty. In an effort to coax some turn from the pitch, Ironmonger dropped his pace and bowled a little fuller, only for both Roach and Martinto drive him for four.

Grimmett made the first breakthrough with a quicker top-spinner that hurried through to catch Roach in front of his stumps. But Headley settled in quickly, playing strokes all round the ground, and picking up two unearned runs when Ironmonger missed with a clumsy attempt to field a ball with his feet. When Fairfax was reintroduced to the attack, Headley cracked fours through point and square leg. He would have collected a third boundary in the over, had his straight drive not been stopped by the stumps at the bowler's end. He reached fifty in just over an hour, and carried on unfurling his strokes, relishing the opportunity to play an attacking innings, instead of retrieving a collapse. Martin, wisely, settled for a supporting role, but it was his cover drive for four from Grimmett that raised the century partnership in only 90 minutes.

Headley's first real error came after tea when, on 95, he edged Fairfax to slip and the catch was turfed by Keith Rigg, who had replaced Jackson in the eleven after four Tests as twelfth man. A few balls later, Headley glanced Ironmonger for two runs to raise his century after batting for just over two hours. He didn't last much longer, playing around a straight ball from Stan McCabe, but he had given the Sydney crowd a demonstration of his real capabilities – and placed his team in an extremely strong position.

Jack Grant had played throughout the tour as a dutiful blocker: now, going in at 222 for two, he had the rare chance to take the initiative. In the hour before stumps he cracked 48 runs, mostly hitting off the back foot, but occasionally advancing down the pitch to attack the spinners. Martin simply continued batting, waiting for a chance to pick off a short or overpitched delivery. He pushed a single to reach his century, promptly appealed against the light, and walked from the field with the score on 299 for two.

And then it rained. Not too heavily, but persistently. The pitch was uncovered, except for the bowlers' footholds, and there was no play before lunch on the second day. When the game resumed, Fairfax found enough spite in the surface to strike Grant a couple of unpleasant blows, before the West Indian captain nudged a single to bring up his half century. Runs were hard to come by, although Ironmonger twice dropped short, Martin pulling each long-hop to the fence. Grant decided to attack the left-armer, too, pulling and driving him for successive fours before edging an over-optimistic heave to McCabe. Sealy, Constantine and Bartlett evidently had instructions to force the pace, and all three fell in quick succession. When Grimmett took the ball to deliver his 33rd over of the innings, Grant walked onto the field and signalled that it would be the last. Obediently following instructions, Frank Martin lashed out at the last ball of the over, only to sky the ball high to mid on – and Bert Ironmonger. Ironmonger circled hopefully beneath the ball, going through all the motions of a man who planned to catch it, while Bradman and Ponsford sprinted across from cover and mid-wicket, desperate to reach the ball before Ironmonger could. It dropped to the ground between the three of them, while the batsmen completed two runs. The West Indies closed their innings at 350 for six, with Frank Martin unbeaten on 123.

George Francis had toiled away quietly for the whole of the tour, working hard on pitches that offered him nothing, bowling his off-stump line and maintaining a respectable pace. Now, at last, he had a chance to exploit a helpful surface, on which the ball was beginning to lift sharply. He gave Bill Ponsford a short ball, which the batsman hooked away for two, and followed it with a fuller delivery that jumped, which Ponsford could only fend away to Bartlett at backward square-leg.

Bill Woodfull dropped anchor. Don Bradman attacked. Frank Martin's match became increasingly surreal. First he had defied Australia's best bowlers for almost six hours, and now he was bowling to Bradman – Bradman! – with two slips, a silly point and a silly mid-off. Attempting a rare attacking stroke, Woodfull was hopelessly beaten by Martin, only for Barrow to fumble the chance of a stumping. Bradman decided to push the field out, and cracked some fierce strokes in Grant's direction, until the captain pushed back a yard or two at silly point. After racing to 43, at the rate of almost a run a minute, Bradman drove loosely at Martin, and George Francis, at slip, dived full length to grab the ball in his right hand. Constantine, who was troubled by a sore shoulder, then removed Alan Kippax thanks to a smart slip catch by Sealy. Keith Rigg's first Test innings lasted for 25 minutes before he edged a leg-side delivery from Francis to Ivan Barrow, and Woodfull's long vigil ended when Constantine made an excellent catch at slip from Martin's bowling. By the time the umpires decided that the light was too poor for play to continue, the Australians had lost five wickets for 89 runs.

Bat used by Don Bradman to score 223 against the West Indies in Brisbane sold for $165,000 in Adelaide in March 2024.

8

March

The West Indies claim the 'fifth Test Ashes'; Waterline springs a surprise; Don Bradman visits the dentist; and the Australian Labor Party shoots itself in the foot.

The first day of March was a Sunday, the rest day in the Test. It was bad timing for the West Indians, because by Monday morning, the SCG pitch had dried out into a flat, easy strip. Stan McCabe and Alan Fairfax found the conditions so comfortable that, in the first half hour of the day, they added 41 runs to the score. But the tireless Francis then broke through twice in quick succession: McCabe pulled a bouncer straight to Headley at square leg, and Ron Oxenham nicked a catch to Ivan Barrow, standing well back. Then Constantine troubled Bert Oldfield with a short delivery, which caught the top edge of his bat, but Barrow mistimed his leap and the ball sailed past him. Oldfield and Fairfax then settled into a stubborn partnership, in which the wicket-keeper did most of the scoring. It took another error by Ivan Barrow to break the stand. A ball from Tommy Scott eluded his gloves, and Bert Oldfield misjudged how far it had run; attempting a second bye, he was run out. That exposed the tail to the West Indian fast bowlers, and the Australian innings was soon over, 130 runs behind the visitors.

The match was, at least in theory, timeless, and the West Indians could have tried to bat Australia out of the game. Instead, Jack Grant decided that they should gather runs as quickly as possible. Martin moved quickly to 20 before falling to Grimmett; in this match, it had taken the Australians more than six and a half hours to earn his wicket. Roach and Headley played bright, short innings; Grant swiped effectively, Constantine recklessly; and Sealy was run out, backing up too far in the search for stolen runs. At stumps, the West Indies were 124 for five, having extended their lead to no more than 254. It looked tactically naïve; there was now every chance that they would be bowled out, leading by less than 300, which was not an intimidating target for Australia's batsmen. But Grant had one eye on the weather forecast, and he knew that more rain was coming.

When it rained, it rained relentlessly, and the whole of Tuesday's play was lost. From early on Wednesday morning, the sun shone brightly, and it was clear that the pitch would be awkward. And Jack Grant, usually the most overcautious of overthinkers, did something no Test captain had ever done before: he declared his team's innings closed for the second time in the match. 'Opinions differed', Grant later recalled, but 'I decided on the bolder alternative – namely, not to go on batting.' Never before had a Test captain set a team containing Bradman a target as modest as 254. The last time a third-innings declaration had set Australia a target had been in Bradman's very first Test, at Brisbane in 1928-29, when England had invited Australia to chase the small matter of 742 runs to win the match.

Francis and Constantine opened the bowling, and in a few frenetic minutes, the West Indies did their best to fumble away their opportunity. Woodfull hadn't scored when he edged Francis low to slip, where Headley dropped the ball. Ponsford had made two runs when he nicked a fast, lifting delivery to Barrow, only for the ball to slip through the wicket-keeper's gloves and ricochet away off his forehead. In the next over, Woodfull edged Francis into the slips again, and this time the diving Sealy barely touched the ball with his outstretched fingers. 'The fact was', Constantine remembered, 'that we were horribly nervous and strung up. And you should have heard them yell on the Hill!'

Constantine bowled beautifully, repeatedly beating the bat but narrowly missing the stumps. But the score mounted steadily. When Martin took the ball, Woodfull relished the opportunity to free his arms, and cracked a drive through cover for four. Woodfull now looked well settled, except when Ponsford slapped a firm drive straight at him, and he was unable to avoid the ball, which hit him either 'in the groin' or 'above the heart', depending on which report you believe. Even though it took Woodfull a while to regain his composure, the openers needed only 53 minutes to reduce the target by 49 runs.

Possibly Woodfull became overconfident. Swinging at a shorter ball from Griffith, he top-edged it straight up into the air. Ivan Barrow was standing almost underneath the ball, wearing gloves, but Barrow wasn't the fieldsman the West Indians trusted in a crisis. As Constantine recalled, 'Everyone yelled, "Learie!" It was a wicket-keeper's catch, but they had called to me and I went to it – got the sun right in my eyes and lost sight of the ball. My heart stopped. I could hear the scream from the stands, and I could not see the ball. I twitched at my cap, got some shade, saw the ball almost down, grabbed it. I found I was trembling so that I could hardly throw it back to the wicket-keeper afterwards.'

Constantine wasn't done. 'In Martin's very next over', according to Jack Grant, 'Learie Constantine came over to me at deep mid off from his position at short mid off and said pleadingly, "Skipper, change places with me." I did not hesitate, for I could trust his judgment in these matters. Once again Ponsford swung at Martin and this time the ball went soaring over the place where I had been, but not where Constantine was. He had retreated several paces towards the boundary, and there he was chasing the flying ball. He caught it magnificently with one hand and threw it what seemed to be 100 yards in the air.'

But still there was Bradman. Grant had learned that Bradman liked to score early in his innings, getting off the mark by tucking the ball away for a single. So he crowded him, with a ring of fieldsmen tasked with preventing a single. Bradman's 'face was as hard as rock', Constantine wrote, 'and he glanced round at us all, giving me the benefit of a specially cold, calculating look.' Herman Griffith did his part, tying Bradman up, not allowing the single, rapping him on the thigh. Martin sent down a maiden to Kippax, and then it was Griffith again, bowling to Bradman. The first ball passed harmlessly outside leg stump, the next outside off. Exactly what happened next isn't clear. Jack Grant thought that Griffith 'held back his second ball' so that 'Bradman, mistaking it in flight, played too soon and dragged it on to his wicket.' The *Sun* told its readers that Bradman 'hit over the ball and was clean bowled'. Constantine believed that Bradman failed to connect, but *The Referee* agreed with Grant that he 'swung wildly, failed to connect properly, and touched the ball into the stumps.' However it happened, the outcome was the same: Bradman was dismissed without scoring for the first time in his Test career.

Bert Oldfield was sent in next, in the hope that he could soak up time to allow the pitch to improve. It wasn't a terrible plan, but it didn't work: Oldfield missed his first ball, and was given out lbw. Australia had lost four wickets for four runs. All the momentum now was with the West Indies, and Constantine made Alan Kippax struggle dreadfully, beating him time after time until, eventually, he turned a fast off-break into the hands of Roach at square leg. Keith Rigg found his Test debut a harsher initiation than he had expected, but survived to the lunch break, when the score was

74 for five. He didn't last much longer, though: he tried to hook Constantine, but only succeeded in looping the gentlest of catches to Ivan Barrow. With two vivid catches and two quick wickets, Constantine had – for the first time in the series – placed his stamp upon the game. His tail was up; the pace of one short delivery surprised Alan Fairfax so much that it knocked his bat out of his hands.

Even so, the pitch had eased noticeably during the lunch interval, and when Rigg was dismissed, Stan McCabe was joined by Alan Fairfax – and Archie Jackson, who acted as runner for Fairfax, who had a bruised heel. McCabe was in a pugnacious mood, driving and pulling with tremendous power, while Fairfax defended grimly. The score mounted. Tommy Scott was called up, but made no impact. Griffith bowled an expensive over. The match was still a contest. Constantine thought he had Fairfax lbw when he struck the batsman on the toe; Martin thought exactly the same thing in the next over, but both appeals were rejected.

McCabe and Fairfax added 79 runs in just over an hour: the Australians needed only 96 more. Then McCabe checked a drive at Martin, and mishit the ball straight to Grant at mid-off. It was the critical breakthrough. Frank Martin, the cashier for the United Fruit Company, the 'portly veteran' who 'wouldn't get a game for Paddington', had scored 143 runs in the Test, had lost his wicket only once, and had now dismissed Bradman, Ponsford, Woodfull and McCabe.

Alan Fairfax fought on. He had only the bowlers for company, and he looked to attack more. He jumped out of his crease to attack Scott, and missed – but so did Ivan Barrow, and the stumping chance went begging. Now the target was down to 70. But in the last over before tea, Scott rapped Oxenham on the pad, and this time the umpire agreed with the appeal.

Clarrie Grimmett was his team's last real hope. He wasn't a negligible batsman, and had made a half-century against the West Indians earlier in the tour. He played sensibly, defending carefully and picking up runs whenever the ball was wide of the stumps. In less than half an hour, he and Fairfax cut the target in half. Grant recalled Griffith, who dropped the first ball of his new spell short outside the off stump, and Grimmett slashed at it, hard. The ball flew high and fast to point, where Constantine leapt into the air and pulled down a spectacular catch.

No one expected Bert Ironmonger to last very long. His batting was notoriously inept. By this late stage of his career, his batting had been reduced to two strokes – a defensive prod, and a crooked drive that could send the ball anywhere on the field, depending mostly on the speed and direction of the ball. But he did his best to keep Fairfax company, poking the ball away for a two, and a couple of singles. Australia's slim chances depended on Fairfax keeping the strike. As Grant recalled, Griffith then bowled to Ironmonger, and 'the second ball hit him on his pads and trickled off in the general direction of square leg.' Grant remembered Fairfax calling for the run and heading down the pitch, but that was actually done by Fairfax's runner, Jackson – Fairfax was hobbling beside the square leg umpire. In any case, 'there was now a three-sided chase – a fieldsman to pick up the ball and throw it to the bowler's end; myself to get to the bowler's end to receive the ball; and Ironmonger to get to the bowler's end in time.' Grant collected Frank Martin's return, and knocked off the bails with Ironmonger, a lumbering mover, well short of his ground. Grant held onto the ball, which he later had mounted and engraved as a souvenir.

When the last wicket fell, Learie Constantine looked around the ground and saw that 'the Hill turned white with whirling waved newspapers and sunhats like a vast bank of flowers bursting into bloom in the tropic sun.'

§

Once Australia had lost a Test match and Bradman had made a duck, perhaps it was inevitable that Phar Lap would lose a race. He had won two events in the first week of the VRC's autumn meeting at Flemington, extending his winning streak to fourteen, but Tommy Woodcock thought he was over-raced and unwell. 'I found when we arrived at his stable that he tore into his feed ravenously' Woodcock recalled, 'and that was the sure sign that he was tired of racing. I suggested a spell. But there were a few more plums to be picked up.' In the CM Lloyd Stakes, run over one mile, Phar Lap was asked to carry 9 stone 7 pounds – significantly more than his nearest rival, Waterline, who was given 8 stone. Only four horses started the race, with Phar Lap the strong favourite at three to one on. Phar Lap was, again, slow to start, and at one point was six lengths behind the early leader, Temoin. He had taken the lead by the final furlong, and the race became a sprint between Phar Lap and Waterline. Waterline made it home by a neck.

§

Harry Mallett spent his last few days in Australia wrangling with his hosts over money. Right at the end of the tour, it dawned on Joe Scheult that the West Indians had been receiving less than half of the gate receipts from their matches. It's alarming that it took Scheult, an experienced bank manager, so long to identify this issue, since the only skill it required was the ability to divide by two. Mallett wrote to the Australian Board of Control to complain about the underpayment, only to be told that he should read the tour contract. The agreement between the two Boards provided that the West Indies were to receive half of the gate receipts, but 'calculated by reference to the price for the outer ground.' In other words, if a spectator paid three shillings for a seat in a grandstand, the West Indies' 'half' of that payment was assessed as if only one shilling and sixpence had been paid. Mallett, who thought this was a sleight of hand, was unimpressed, but the Australian Board refused to budge. Nor was it prepared to increase the amount of its tour guarantee to reflect the fact that the Australian pound had lost a quarter of its value. The one concession the Australian Board offered was to defer paying its guarantee until some indefinite time in the future when the exchange rate might have improved.

§

At the start of the series, Don Bradman's batting average in Test cricket stood at 103. Against the West Indies, he averaged no more than 74. That was still exceptional, but at least it proved that Bradman was occasionally fallible. It was as if Phar Lap lost every fourth race.

'We were up against a much better side than ourselves', George Headley admitted. 'There was no question about that.' Yet he believed that the West Indians would have done better, but for the fact that 'one had to fight hard for his runs, and quite a few of the West Indies side lacked that fighting spirit.' Fighting spirit, Headley thought, came from team spirit, but 'it is hard for us to get going as a team.' He wondered what a more united West Indies team might have accomplished – especially on faster pitches.

It would take twelve months before the West Indians' performance could be placed into proper perspective: by then, Australia had demolished the touring South Africans by winning all five Tests of their series. One match was won by ten wickets, and three by an innings and more than one hundred runs. Bradman averaged 201.50 with the bat and Bert Ironmonger took 31 wickets at an average of nine. Helped, admittedly, by a wet pitch, Ironmonger routed South Africa for 36 and 45 in the last Test in Melbourne. The South Africans were a vastly more experienced team than the West Indies, whose efforts in containing Australia's batting strength, and winning a Test on their first tour of the country, began to look more impressive in retrospect.

§

The New South Wales Cricket Association hosted a farewell lunch for the West Indians at the Hotel Sydney. Jack Grant made his last speech of the tour, joking that his team 'was taking back the fifth Test Ashes!' Several minor local cricketing dignitaries competed to shower the tourists with condescendingly faint praise. 'You came here as strangers', said Ron Jones of the NSWCA, 'We feel sure that on your next trip your finances will be happier. Your performances on the field were not a true reflection of your worth.' Aub Oxlade, representing the Australian Board of Control, remarked that 'we have had many teams here, but never one that has given us less trouble.' The acting President of the NSWCA, Alfred Green, observed that 'when Bradman was out for a duck, perhaps you shared in our surprise.' The West Indians responded as if one more meal accompanied by patronising speeches was exactly what they wanted.

The West Indians sailed for New Zealand on the Maunganui on the afternoon of 6 March 1931 – all except for Jack Grant, who instead headed to Melbourne to catch a ship to Bombay, on his way to meet Ida in Rhodesia. Joe Scheult took with him some unusual souvenirs – two wallabies, provided to him by a trustee of Taronga Zoo in Sydney, and two kookaburras, the gift of 'a friend in Adelaide'. Usually, the export of native fauna was prohibited, but Scheult somehow obtained permission for his cargo from the Controller of Customs. The male wallaby died soon after reaching Trinidad, but the other creatures thrived, at least for a time.

The return voyage was mercifully free from storms.

§

On the Friday after the Sydney Test, Don Bradman went to the dentist and had some teeth extracted. This was big news in Sydney, although the papers were divided on the vital question of whether five teeth had been removed, or only two. His doctor ordered him to rest, but Bradman ignored that advice and played the next day for his club, St George. Because he was still feeling sore, he didn't bat until St George, chasing Marrickville's 109, had lost seven wickets for 60 runs. By the close of play, he had reached eight; in just over an hour on the following Saturday, he took his score to 116 not out.

§

There was one tour left in the season. Alan Kippax assembled a team of players from New South Wales to travel around the Queensland countryside, playing exhibition games against local teams. These matches attracted big crowds, since it was the only opportunity many people in those areas would have to see Kippax, Archie Jackson, Don Bradman, Stan McCabe and Alan Fairfax in action. The players each received £50 for the tour, which was tidy money for a couple of weeks of smashing runs against rustic cricketers.

Archie Jackson was in rich form, cracking 171 at Townsville and pulverising the bowling wherever he went. He found it exhausting, but he couldn't stop scoring runs. And a visit to Queensland meant a visit to Phyllis. He continued planning for the future he would never enjoy, writing a letter to Bill Hunt during the tour in which he asked 'Have you arranged our wedding, or merely fixed our engagement? However I am still interested. After all it is most likely worth exploring.'

Archie Jackson's engagement to Phyllis Thomas was announced on 16 February 1933, a few hours before his death.

§

On 14 March, the Sydney metropolitan conference of the Labor Party voted unanimously to expel the Federal Treasurer, Ted Theodore.

The motion proposed that 'Mr Theodore, by his public declaration, in which he falsely described Labor's policy of reconstruction as "muddle-headed policy of repudiation", and in which he said that he would not hold himself subject to the authority of the

New South Wales Labor movement; and by his action in inciting other members of the Federal Labor Party to reject the authority of the New South Wales executive, has by such conduct placed himself outside the Labor movement.'

Since Theodore was not a member of the Sydney branch, the motion was merely symbolic. Its author was Jack Lang, who sensed that Scullin was a vulnerable leader and that, should the Prime Minister fall, the urbane Theodore was Lang's strongest challenger for leadership of the party. 'At the Trades Hall', one journalist observed, 'it is recognised that it is now war to the political death between these two.' But the greatest casualty was the Labor Party. Almost two weeks later, delegates assembled in Sydney for a national conference of the Labor Party – which was boycotted by Lang and his supporters. Lang's bid to win control of the party only had the effect of splitting it in two.

But why split in two, when you can split in three? It would be wrong to say that the Scullin government had no plan for tackling the Depression. It had at least two – it just couldn't agree within itself on which one was better. As Federal Treasurer, Ted Theodore had argued for increased government spending to stimulate the economy, while his disappointed rival, Joe Lyons, had urged Scullin to cut the federal budget and reduce government salaries. Lyons had already stormed out of cabinet in protest at Theodore's reinstatement; in March, along with five other Labor members, Lyons quit the party altogether, crossing the floor to sit with the opposition. Shortly afterwards, he assumed the leadership of a new conservative party – the United Australia Party. What had been, at the start of the year, the Labor Party, was now the Labor Party, Lang Labor and a faction of the UAP.

Not only did the fractures in the party fail to deliver to Lang the leadership he coveted, they were also to consign Labor to opposition for almost ten years.

§

During the cricket season Alan Fairfax was rewarded generously for playing the game he loved. When it ended, he was confronted with the grim reality of his life – that he was unemployed, about to be married, had few skills that were marketable in a depression, and would make no money from cricket during the winter. Before the tour to England, he had worked as a sporting goods salesman, but he was unable to find any work of that kind upon his return.

Fairfax had played in ten of Australia's eleven Tests since making his debut against England in March 1929. He averaged 51.25 with the bat, and bowled well enough to be entrusted with the new ball. Although he was a far less spectacular cricketer than Constantine, he was arguably the most effective Test all-rounder in the world, and he was still only twenty-four years old, his potential barely tapped. But none of that generated a secure income. He began discussions with a number of Lancashire League clubs, and eventually signed a three-year contract with Accrington, worth £20 a week. No one involved in the administration of Australian cricket did anything to prevent him leaving. In the Sydney Test against the West Indies, Fairfax had opened the bowling and top-scored in each innings, but he played only twice more for New South Wales and never appeared again in Test cricket.

§

Before he left Sydney, Errol Hunte provided one last article to the Australian press – a summary of his visit, which was published in *The Referee.* 'Everything in Australia', he observed, 'seems to be staged on the grand scale, even the depression. We are deeply in sympathy with you, and fervently hope the time is not too far distant when your country will rise, like the phoenix, from the ashes of her present lean period.'

Australia v West Indies

Sydney Cricket Ground, 27, 28 February, 2, 3, 4 March 1931

Umpires: HJ Armstrong, WG French

West Indies won by 30 runs

West Indies

FR Martin	not out	123	c McCabe b Grimmett	20
CA Roach	lbw b Grimmett	31	c Oldfield b Grimmett	34
GA Headley	lbw b McCabe	105	b Oxenham	30
GC Grant	c McCabe b Ironmonger	62	not out	27
JED Sealy	c Kippax b Grimmett	4	run out	7
LN Constantine	c McCabe b Ironmonger	0	c Bradman b Ironmonger	4
EL Bartlett	b Grimmett	0	not out	0
IM Barrow	not out	7		
OC Scott				
GN Francis				
HC Griffith				
Extras	(6 b, 5 lb, 6 nb, 1 w)	18	(1 b, 1 lb)	2
Total	(6 declared)	350	(5 declared)	124

Bowling

	Overs	Mdns	Runs	Wkts		Overs	Mdns	Runs	Wkts
Fairfax	21	2	60	0		-	-	-	-
Oxenham	24	10	51	0		10	4	14	1
Ironmonger	42	16	95	2		16	7	44	2
Grimmett	33	7	100	3		18	4	47	1
McCabe	15	5	26	1		7	2	17	0

Australia

WM Woodfull	c Constantine b Martin	22	c Constantine b Griffith	18
WH Ponsford	c Bartlett b Francis	7	c Constantine b Martin	28
DG Bradman	c Francis b Martin	43	b Griffith	0
AF Kippax	c Sealy b Constantine	3	c Roach b Constantine	10
KE Rigg	c Barrow b Francis	14	c Barrow b Constantine	16
SJ McCabe	c Headley b Francis	21	c Grant b Martin	44
AG Fairfax	st Barrow b Scott	54	not out	60
RK Oxenham	c Barrow b Francis	0	lbw b Scott	14
WAS Oldfield	run out	36	lbw b Griffith	0
CV Grimmett	not out	15	c Constantine b Griffith	12
H Ironmonger	b Griffith	1	run out	4
Extras	(1 b, 7 lb)	8	(3 b, 7 lb, 2 nb, 2 w)	14
Total		224	(0 wickets)	220

Bowling

	Overs	Mdns	Runs	Wkts		Overs	Mdns	Runs	Wkts
Francis	19	6	48	4		16	2	32	0
Griffith	13.2	3	31	1		13.3	3	50	4
Martin	27	3	67	2		18	4	44	2
Constantine	10	2	28	1		17	2	50	2
Scott	10	1	42	1		11	-	30	1

Epilogue: the players

Ivan Barrow retained his place as the West Indies' first-choice wicket-keeper on the 1933 tour to England. At Manchester, he became the first West Indian to score a Test century in England – but only narrowly, because George Headley was at the other end, on 99, when Barrow reached three figures. In 1934-35, Barrow was displaced behind the stumps by the brilliant Cyril Christiani of British Guiana, but after Christiani's tragic early death from malaria, Barrow was recalled to tour England in 1939. He worked for many years for the Jamaican Development Corporation, later becoming a director of a manufacturing company. He was a prominent figure in Jamaican horse racing; for more than a decade, he was the official handicapper for events conducted by the Turf Club of Jamaica, and he was the first man to provide live radio commentary of horse racing in Jamaica. He is one of the six Test wicket-keepers to have attended Wolmer's School in Jamaica, the others being Karl Nunes, Gerry Alexander, Jackie Hendriks, Jeff Dujon and Carlton Baugh.

Ivanhoe Mordecai Barrow was born in Morant Bay, Jamaica, on 16 January 1911 and died at Kingston on 2 April 1979. In 11 Tests between 1929-30 and 1939, he scored 276 runs at 16.23, held 17 catches and completed 5 stumpings. He played 68 first-class matches between 1928-29 and 1946, scoring 2551 runs at 23.84, holding 73 catches and completing 27 stumpings. He conceded 34 runs with the ball without taking a wicket. The highest of his three centuries was 169 for Jamaica against Lord Tennyson's XI in 1931-32.

The innings of 84 **Edward Bartlett** played on his Test debut turned out to be the high point of his career. He never again reached fifty in a first-class match, although he continued to play for Barbados until 1938-39. For reasons no-one understands, Wisden erroneously published his obituary in 1934, some 42 years before he actually died. In 1988, Barbados issued a 50 cent postage stamp featuring Herman Griffith, 101 of which accidentally showed a picture of Bartlett instead of Griffith.

Edward Lawson Bartlett was born at St Michaels, Barbados, on 10 March 1906 and died at St Michaels, Barbados, on 21 December 1976. In five Tests, he scored 131 runs at 18.71 and held two catches. In 42 first-class matches between 1923-24 and 1938-39, he scored 1581 runs at 23.25, and

Barrow drops Woofull watched by Constantine and Francis.

George Francis in the nets.

held 8 catches. His only century was 109 for the West Indians against Nottinghamshire in 1928.

Lionel Birkett played no more Test cricket after the Australian tour, as he withdrew from first-class cricket for seven years to concentrate on his career as a chemist in the sugar industry. When he eventually resumed his first-class career, as captain of Trinidad, he hit 121 against British Guiana in his first game back. He later moved to Berbice and his final match, in September 1944, was for British Guiana. His expertise in sugar production technology was in high demand, and he published numerous scholarly papers on the subject, with titles like 'A Review of Fertilizer and Manurial Experiments on Sugar-cane production in British Guiana, 1930-1953' and 'An Index of Relative Fertility of Cane Fields'. Immediately before his death he had been the oldest living Test cricketer from any country.

Lionel Sydney Birkett was born at St Michael, Barbados, on 14 April 1905, and died at St James, Barbados, on 16 January 1998. In 4 Test matches he scored 136 runs at 17.00, held 4 catches, and took one wicket for 71 runs. In 26 first-class matches between 1924-25 and 1944-45, he scored 1295 runs at 33.20 (with three centuries), held 22 catches and took 9 wickets at 56.00.

It could be argued that, for a player of such spectacular talent, **Learie Constantine** underachieved as a Test cricketer, but that could not be said of his life as a whole. He eventually achieved his ambition to become a lawyer in 1954, when he was called to the bar at Middle Temple. In the meantime, he had worked as a welfare office in the Ministry of Labour and National Service, and received the MBE for his work with the Ministry during the war. In 1943, he successfully sued the Imperial Hotel in London for refusing to lodge him and his family on the ground of their colour. He became an active campaigner for civil rights for people of colour, and published a polemical account of his experiences of racial prejudice, Colour Bar. Returning to Trinidad in 1954, he was elected to Parliament and became Minister of Communications, Works and Utilities. When he chose not to seek re-election in 1961, he was appointed Trinidad's High Commissioner to London, a post he held for three years. He was knighted in 1962, served as a governor of the BBC and then, awarded a life peerage in 1969, became the first black man to sit in the House of Lords.

Learie Nicholas Constantine was born at Diego Martin, Trinidad on 21 September 1901, and died at London on 1 July 1971. In 18 Tests he scored 635 runs at 19.24, held 28 catches and took 58 wickets at 30.10. His highest score was 90 against England at Port of Spain in 1934-35, and in his last Test, against England at The Oval in 1939, he hit 79 and took 5-75. In 119 first-class matches between 1921-22 and 1945, he scored 4475 runs at 24.05 (with five centuries) and took 439 wickets at 20.48. In his final first-class match, he was captain of The Dominions against England at Lord's. Between 1929 and 1942, he took 799 wickets for Nelson in the Lancashire League.

Frank de Caires returned to Georgetown to work in the family business, of which he remained a director until his early death from bowel cancer at the age of 49. He continued to play for British Guiana until 1938, although he was never again close to selection for the West Indies, despite scoring 80 not out against the touring MCC team in 1934-35. His son, David, became a lawyer, and later a prominent, fiercely independent journalist (who founded the Stabroek News); his grand-daughter, Isabelle, is a trustee of the Moray House Trust (which promotes Guyanese culture and public discourse) and married Michael Atherton; and his great-grandson, Joshua de Caires, has opened the batting for Middlesex. The de Caires family and the Wight family remain friends to this day.

Francis Ignatius de Caires was born in Guyana on 12 May 1909 and died in Guyana on 2 February 1959. He played three Test matches, scoring 232 runs at 38.66, holding one catch and conceding 9 runs without taking a wicket. In 18 first-class matches between 1928-29 and 1938, he scored 945 runs at 28.63 (with one century), held 7 catches and took one wicket for 48 runs.

George Francis played only two first-class games after the Australian tour, his last being the Test at Lord's in 1933. In 1933 and 1934, he was the professional for the Radcliffe Club in the Bolton League.

George Nathaniel Francis was born on 11 December 1897 at St James, Barbados, and died on 12 January 1942 at Black Rock, Barbados. In 10 Tests, he scored 81 runs at 5.78, held 7 catches and took 23 wickets at 33.17. In 62 first-class matches between 1923 and 1933, he scored 874 runs at 12.85, held 42 catches and took 223 wickets at 23.13. His best return with the ball was 7-50 for Barbados against MCC in 1925-26.

Jack Grant continued to lead the West Indies in two more Test series, leading the side to a series victory over England in 1934-35, before retiring from Test cricket at the age of 27. In 1931-32, he played for Rhodesia in the Currie Cup, which meant that he played first-class cricket in England, Australia and South Africa before appearing anywhere in the West Indies. Although he was nominally a Trinidad cricketer, his first match for the island (and he played no more than four) was his 74th appearance in first-class cricket. In the final Test of the 1934-35 series, he left the field with an injury and, in the absence of an official vice-captain, deputed the leadership to Learie Constantine, who was at the helm when the game was won. He married Ida Russell, in Southern Rhodesia, on precisely the same day that his twin sister married in Canada. Grant began his career as a schoolmaster at Plumtree School and Milton College, in Southern Rhodesia; from there, he returned to Queens Royal College in Port of Spain, where he worked until 1935. He then became Principal of the Grenada Boys' Secondary School. The Colonial Education Service transferred him to Zanzibar in 1944, a position he did not enjoy, partly because he did not feel accepted by the only Protestant church on the island. Upon his resignation, he was offered a position at Adams College near Durban. Adams College was an independent school for black students, and Grant found himself facing stern opposition from the government, which instructed the school to provide 'education for natives as an independent race' – that is, to implement apartheid, which Grant abhorred and publicly opposed. In 1954, the government determined that teacher training courses, such as the one Adams College offered, could be provided only by the state, and two years later, after relentless government pressure, Adams College was liquidated. Grant spent some years performing various missionary roles in Africa, and in 1961, he established the first private multi-racial school in Rhodesia, at Chikore, originally for the purpose of educating the children of missionaries. He was frequently in conflict with the government led by Ian Smith, and in 1975, he and Ida were declared prohibited immigrants. They returned to Cambridge, where they had met, and where Grant died suddenly at the age of 68.

George Copeland Grant was born on 9 May 1907 at Port of Spain and died at Cambridge, England on 26 October 1978. In 12 Tests between 1930-31 and 1934-35, he scored 413 runs at 25.81, held 10 catches and conceded 18 runs without taking a wicket. In 81 first-class matches between 1928 and 1934-35, he scored 3831 runs at 32.19, held 71 catches, and took 19 wickets at 51.00. The highest of his four centuries was 115 for the West Indians against an England XI at Folkestone in 1933, when he shared a third-wicket partnership of 226 with George Headley.

Herman Griffith played the last of his Test matches in England in 1933, when he was forty years of age. When he was 47, he became the first black man to captain Barbados, and was still effective enough with the ball to take 3-38 against Trinidad. He became the Chief Sanitary Inspector of Barbados.

Herman Clarence Griffith was born at Arima, Trinidad on 1 December 1893 and died at Bridgetown on 18 March 1980. In 13 Tests, he scored 91 runs at 5.05, held four catches and took 44 wickets at 28.25. In 79 first-class matches between 1921-22 and 1940-41, he scored 1204 runs at 15.05, held 36 catches and took 258 wickets at 28.27. He took 7-38 on his debut for Barbados against Trinidad in 1921-22, figures which remained his best in first-class matches.

George Headley became one of the greatest batsmen ever produced by the West Indies. In the years between 1930 and 1939, when he sometimes appeared to carry his team's batting single-handedly, he averaged almost 67 in Test cricket. He toured England twice, scoring 2320 first-class runs at 66.28 in 1933 and 1745 runs at 72.70 in 1939. His stature was acknowledged in 1948 when, in the first Test against England, he became the first black man to be appointed to captain the West Indies. In 1955, he was appointed the Jamaican national cricket coach, and he was awarded the MBE in 1956. His son, Ron, played Test cricket for the West Indies in 1973, and his grandson, Dean, opened the bowling for England.

George Alphonso Headley was born at Colon, Panama, on 30 May 1909 and died at Kingston, Jamaica on 30 November 1983. In 22 Tests between 1929-30 and 1953-54, he scored 2190 runs at 60.83 (with 10 centuries), held 14 catches and conceded 230 runs without taking a wicket. His highest score was 270 not out against England at Kingston in 1934-35. In 103 first-class matches between 1927-28 and 1954, he hit 9921 runs at 69.86, held 76 catches, and took 51 wickets at 36.11. The highest of his 33 centuries was 344 not out for Jamaica against Lord Tennyson's XI in 1931-32, his first match in first-class cricket after the tour to Australia.

Errol Hunte played only three more matches for Trinidad after the Australian tour, and never again represented the West Indies. He became a prominent civil servant in Trinidad, serving as the Principal Officer of the District Administration of St Patrick county and as the Director of Social and Community Development in the Ministry of Local Government and Community Development. He was only 57 when he suffered a fatal stroke. For 18 years, Wisden's *Cricketers Almanack* erroneously credited one of his Test appearances to 'RL Hunte'.

Errol Ashton Clairmore Hunte was born at Port of Spain on 3 October 1905, and died at Port of Spain on 26 June 1967. In three Test matches, he scored 166 runs at 33.20 and held 5 catches. In 15 first-class matches between 1928-29 and 1933-34, he scored 472 runs at 20.52, held 29 catches and completed 7 stumpings.

Frank Martin was almost forty years old when he toured England with the West Indians in 1933. Early in the tour he batted usefully and bowled well, but while chasing a ball in the field against Middlesex at Lord's, he collided with the sightscreen and damaged his ankle so badly that he never reappeared in first-class cricket. He served as a selector for the Jamaican cricket team for 21 years.

Frank Reginald Martin was born at Kingston on 12 October 1893 and died at Kingston on 23 November 1967. In 9 Tests he hit 486 runs at 28.58, held two catches, and took 8 wickets at 77.37. In 65 first-class matches between 1924-25 and 1933, he hit 3589 runs at 37.77 (with six centuries), held 19 catches, and took 74 wickets at 52.55. His highest score was 204 not out for Jamaica against Lord Tennyson's XI in 1926-27, and he took 5-90 for the West Indians against Glamorgan in 1933.

Clifford Roach toured England in 1933, when his tally of 1286 first-class runs was second only to Headley. Having been the first West Indian to score a Test century, and the first to record a double-century, he became (at Lord's) the first to record a 'pair' in a Test in England, although he did recover to score 64 in the next Test, at Old Trafford. His last Test was the first match of the 1934-35 series against England, after which he enjoyed a few more successful seasons for Trinidad. His health was precarious in later life; he suffered from arteriosclerosis compounded by diabetes, and his right leg was amputated in 1968, after which the left was removed in 1970, both amputations being performed on 31 July). Nonetheless, he continued to carry on his practice as a solicitor. With his wife Edna, he had nine children. He was the last survivor of the first ever West Indian Test team. He served as a Port of Spain City Councillor and was awarded Trinidad's highest decoration, the Humming Bird Medal (Gold) in 1972. In 1984, he was inducted into the Trinidad and Tobago Sporting Hall of Fame – quite apart from his cricket, he had also been an outstanding footballer, representing Trinidad.

Clifford Archibald Roach was born at Port of Spain on 13 March 1904, and died at Port of Spain on 16 April 1988. In 16 Tests, he scored 952 runs at 30.70 (with two centuries), held 6 catches, and took two wickets at 51.50. In 98 first-class matches between 1923-24 and 1937-38, he scored 4851 runs at 28.04 (with five centuries), held 43 catches, and took five wickets at 105.20.

The tour match against South Australia was **Edwin St Hill**'s final appearance in first-class cricket, after which he played out his career as a peripatetic league professional in northern England. Two months after the tour ended, he began his stint as with Lowerhouse, taking 201 wickets in the next three Lancashire League seasons. In 1934, he accepted a contract worth £240 a year to play for Slaithwaite in the Huddersfield League where, although he was successful on the field, the club struggled to afford his salary. He moved on to East Brierley in the Bradford League, then returned to the Huddersfield League to play for Lascelles Hall. Illness cut his season short, and again he moved on, spending two seasons with Spen Victoria in the Bradford League. When war broke out, he joined the Army, was deployed to France and evacuated from Dunkirk. Discharged from the Army in 1941, he continued to play in various northern leagues until 1952. At the time of his death, he was employed as a clerk in the Ministry of Fuel.

Edwin Lloyd St Hill was born 9 March 1904 at Port of Spain and died on 21 May 1957 in Manchester, England. In two Tests, he scored 18 runs at 4.50 and took 3 wickets at 73.66. In 17 first-class matches between 1923-24 and 1930-31, he scored 274 runs at 11.91 and took 64 wickets at 28.62.

Tommy Scott played only three more matches for Jamaica after the Australian tour, although he remained as effective as ever, taking 21 wickets in those games. When he was in his mid-forties, many Jamaicans continued to argue that he was the best slow bowler on the island, and although he retired from international cricket in 1936, he played on for his club until 1938. After serving as the Principal Warden of St Catherine's District Prison between 1929 and 1943, he established Richmond Farm, the first fenceless prison in Jamaica, based on ideas he had gathered during the Australian tour. He was appointed Jamaica's Superintendent of Prisons in 1952. He had seven children, one of whom, Alfred, was a leg spinner who played four first-class matches for Jamaica and a single Test, against India at Kingston in March 1953.

Oscar Charles Scott was born in Kingston on 14 August 1892 and died at Kingston on 15 June 1961. He played 8 Tests between 1928 and 1930-31, scoring 171 runs at 17.10 and taking 22 wickets at 42.04. In 45 first-class matches between 1910-11 and 1934-35, he scored 1317 runs at 24.38, held 14 catches, and took 182 wickets at 30.52. His highest score was 94 for Jamaica against Barbados in 1924-25, and his best return with the ball was 8-67 for Jamaica against Lord Tennyson's XI in 1927-28.

Almost as soon as he graduated from the institution, **Derek Sealy** was appointed to the staff of Combermere School, even though his sole formal qualification was his Leaving Certificate. At Combermere, he taught and coached the young Frank Worrell. Sealy enjoyed a successful Test series against England in 1934-35, when he contributed to a big West Indies win at Port of Spain by scoring 92 and 35 as well as taking 2-7 with his medium pace. After Cyril Christiani's death, he was called upon to keep wicket again on tour in England in 1939, although by then he preferred to bowl. He enjoyed one spectacular success with the ball: playing for Barbados in March 1942, he caught Trinidad on a wet pitch at Kensington Oval, and took 8-8 from 55 balls as the visitors were routed for only 16. He later moved to Trinidad, for whom, in his last first-class match in February 1949, he hit 112 and 53 against Barbados.

James Edward Derrick Sealy was born at St Michael, Barbados, on 11 September 1912 and died at Palo Seco, Trinidad, on 3 January 1982. In 11 Tests between 1929-30 and 1939, he scored 478 runs at 28.11, held 6 catches, executed one stumping, and took three wickets for 94 runs. In 80 first-class matches between 1928-29 and 1948-49, he scored 3831 runs at 30.40 (with 8 centuries), completed 67 catches and 13 stumpings, and took 63 wickets at 28.60. His highest score was 181 for the West Indians against

Middlesex at Lord's in 1939, where he shared a third-wicket stand of 218 with George Headley.

Oscar Wight's cricket never recovered from the disappointment of the Australian tour. He continued to play for British Guiana, intermittently, until 1938, but averaged only 14 with the bat in that time, and never again reached fifty in first-class cricket. He was successful in business, became a printer and newspaper publisher, had seven children, and was appointed Civil Defence Commissioner for British Guiana in 1942. Something of a patron of the arts in the colony, he helped to establish its first radio station, and the influential literary journal Kyk-Over-Al. He was awarded the MBE in 1946 'for public services in British Guiana'. Four of his cousins played first-class cricket for British Guiana (Peter, the best-known, also had a lengthy career with Somerset), and four of his grandsons played List A cricket for the Cayman Islands.

Oscar Stanley Wight was born in Georgetown on 10 August 1906 and died from cancer at Bury St Edmunds, England, on 13 September 1986. He played 15 first-class matches between 1926-27 and 1938, scoring 570 runs at 23.75, holding 11 catches, and conceding 59 runs without taking a wicket. He scored one century, 103 for British Guiana against Barbados at Bourda in 1929-30.

The West Indians in New Zealand and Australia, 1930-31

Scores

At Basin Reserve, Wellington, 12 and 13 November 1930 (not first-class). Wellington 195 (LN Constantine 6-24) drew with West Indies 4 for 128 (LS Birkett 40 not out, ED Blundell 3-33).

At Sydney, 21, 22, 24 and 25 November 1930. West Indies 188 (CA Roach 43, HC Chilvers 4-84, SJ McCabe 3-23, AG Fairfax 3-42) and 241 (GA Headley 82, LN Constantine 59, HC Chilvers 5-73) lost to New South Wales 206 (DG Bradman 73, LN Constantine 4-43, GN Francis 3-38) and six for 224 (A Jackson 62, FR Martin 3-35) by four wickets.

At Melbourne, 28, 29 November and 1 December 1930. West Indies 212 (GA Headley 131, H Ironmonger 5-87, EL a'Beckett 4-51) and 128 (H Ironmonger 8-31) lost to Victoria 594 (WH Ponsford 187, KE Rigg 126, LS Darling 83, J Ryder 65, BA Barnett 58, HSTL Hendry 44, LN Constantine 5-64) by an innings and 254 runs.

At Adelaide, 5, 6 and 8 December 1930. West Indies 171 (CA Roach 64, CV Grimmett 4-71, TA Carlton 3-42) and 162 (CV Grimmett 5-43, MG Waite 3-46) lost to South Australia 330 (PK Lee 55, TW Wall 53 not out, CV Grimmett 50, CW Walker 45, HC Griffith 3-75) and none for 4 by ten wickets.

At Adelaide, 12, 13, 15 and 16 December 1930. First Test. West Indies 296 and 249 lost to Australia 376 and none for 172 by ten wickets.

At Launceston, 20, 22 and 23 December 1930. Tasmania 184 (AO Burrows 46, LJ Nash 41, EL St Hill 4-57) and 119 (DC Green 45, OC Scott 5-63, HC Griffith 3-20) lost to West Indies 353 (LN Constantine 100, GC Grant 65, JED Sealy 42 not out, AO Burrows 3-67) by an innings and 50 runs.

At Hobart, 24, 25 and 26 December 1930. Tasmania 280 (AO Burrows 54, LJ Nash 53, LN Constantine 6-25) drew with West Indies two declared for 242 (LS Birkett 128 not out, FR Martin 79 not out).

At Sydney, 1, 2, 3 and 5 January 1931. Second Test. Australia 369 beat West indies 107 and 90 by an innings and 172 runs.

At Brisbane, 10, 12, 13 and 14 January 1931. West Indies 309 (LN Constantine 75, LS Birkett 49, CA Roach 42, E Gilbert 5-65) and 265 (LN Constantine 97, LS Birkett 41, EC Benstead 3-57) beat Queensland 167 (VHV Goodwin 60, LN Constantine 4-33, OC Scott 3-46) and 188 (VHV Goodwin 54, LN Constantine 3-23, OC Scott 3-79).

At Brisbane, 16, 17, 19 and 20 January 1931. Third Test. Australia 558 beat West Indies 193 and 148 by an innings and 217 runs.

At Newcastle, 24 and 26 January 1931 (not first-class). New South Wales Country 251 (A Bennett 95, EF O'Brien 50, LN Constantine 4-57) and 147 (LN Constantine 5-24, HC Griffith 3-29) lost to West Indies 399 (LN Constantine 147, GA Headley 65, JED Sealy 60 not out, EL Bartlett 48, LD McGuirk 5-58) by an innings and one run.

At Geelong, 29 and 30 January 1931 (not first-class). Victoria Country 327 (AL Hassett 147 not out, EP Just 51, HC Griffith 3-59, LN Constantine 3-81) drew West Indies 222 (EAC Hunte 50, FI de Caires 49, H Zachariah 5-74, P Williams 3-39) and nine for 216 (LN Constantine 80, FR Martin 57, G Freeman 3-89), (see photograph page 176).

At Melbourne, 31 January, 2, 3 and 4 February 1931. West Indies 495 (CA Roach 104, GC Grant 84, GA Headley 77, FI de Caires 76, FR Martin 44, JED Sealy 41, LE Nagel 4-111, LO Cordner 3-154) and five declared for 238 (GA Headley 113, FI de Caires 64) drew Victoria 325 (FC Fontaine 76, HCA Sandford 70, GM Eaton 43, J Rush 42, GN Francis 4-80, EL St Hill 3-81) and nine for 280 (EK Tolhurst 63, PA Ellis 47, SO Quin 43, FR Martin 3-65, EL St Hill 3-76).

At Adelaide, 7, 9, 10 and 11 February 1931. West Indies 383 (GC Grant 102, GA Headley 75, LN Constantine 63, CV Grimmett 5-144, TA Carlton 3-65) and 208 (GC Grant 42, PK Lee 5-57, CV Grimmett 3-93) lost to South Australia 278 (PK Lee 106, CV Grimmett 54, LN Constantine 4-73, OC Scott 3-69) and nine for 314 (MG Waite 82, AR Lonergan 68, VY Richardson 52, OC Scott 5-100).

At Melbourne, 13 and 14 February 1931. Fourth Test. West Indies 99 and 107 lost to Australia 8 declared for 328 by an innings and 122 runs.

At Sydney, 21, 23, 24 and 25 February 1931. West Indies 339 (GA Headley 70, JED Sealy 58, CA Roach 55, LN Constantine 41, HC Chilvers 3-56) and 9 declared for 403 (LN Constantine 93, JED Sealy 92, OC Scott 67 not out, FR Martin 56, IM Barrow 45, HC Chilvers 3-53) beat New South Wales 190 (OW Bill 41, LN Constantine 6-45) and 466 (AF Kippax 141, SJ McCabe 100, DG Bradman 73, HC Chilvers 43 not out, GN Francis 4-76) by 86 runs.

At Sydney, 27, 28 February, 2, 3 and 4 March 1931. Fifth Test. West Indies six declared for 35 and five declared for 124 beat Australia 224 and 220 by 30 runs.

Test Series Averages
Australia

Batsman	M	Inns	NO	HS	Runs	Av	100	50	C/S
WH Ponsford	5	7	1	183	467	77.83	2	1	-
DG Bradman	5	6	-	223	447	74.50	2	-	4
AG Fairfax	5	6	2	60*	195	48.75	-	2	5
AF Kippax	5	6	-	146	277	46.16	1	1	6
WM Woodfull	5	6	-	83	204	34.00	-	2	1
SJ McCabe	5	6	-	90	196	32.66	-	1	10
A Jackson	4	5	1	70*	124	31.00	-	1	6
WAS Oldfield	5	6	2	38*	90	22.50	-	-	6/7
RK Oxenham	3	4	-	48	62	15.50	-	-	1
KE Rigg	1	2	-	16	30	15.00	-	-	-
CV Grimmett	5	5	1	15*	43	10.75	-	-	2
H Ironmonger	4	4	1	4	10	3.33	-	-	-
A Hurwood	2	2	-	5	5	2.50	-	-	2
TW Wall	1	1	-	0	0	0.00	-	-	2

Bowler	Overs	M	Runs	W	Av	Best	5w
H Ironmonger	153	61	323	22	14.68	7-23	1
DG Bradman	9	1	15	1	15.00	1-8	-
A Hurwood	86.1	28	170	11	15.45	4-22	-
CV Grimmett	239.2	61	593	33	17.96	7-87	2
RK Oxenham	88	35	155	7	22.14	4-39	-
AG Fairfax	85	16	206	7	29.42	4-31	-
SJ McCabe	56	13	126	3	42.00	1-16	-
TW Wall	26	1	84	0	-	-	-

West Indies

Batsman	M	Inns	NO	HS	Runs	Av	100	50	C/S
GC Grant	5	10	4	71*	255	42.50	-	3	3
GA Headley	5	10	1	105	336	37.33	2	-	1
FR Martin	5	10	1	123*	254	28.22	1	-	2
EL Bartlett	4	6	1	84	110	22.00	-	1	2
CA Roach	5	10	-	56	194	19.40	-	1	3
LS Birkett	4	8	-	64	136	17.00	-	1	4
IM Barrow	5	9	1	27	122	15.25	-	-	9
OC Scott	5	8	2	20*	89	14.83	-	-	-
JED Sealy	2	4	1	16*	30	10.00	-	-	2
LN Constantine	5	10	-	14	72	7.20	-	-	9
HC Griffith	5	8	-	12	43	5.37	-	-	-
GN Francis	5	8	1	8	31	4.42	-	-	3

Bowler	Overs	M	Runs	W	Av	Best	5w
HC Griffith	133.5	20	393	14	28.07	4-50	-
GN Francis	129	23	350	11	31.81	4-48	-
OC Scott	105.3	4	448	11	40.72	4-66	-
LN Constantine	127.3	15	407	8	50.87	2-50	-
FR Martin	160.2	17	448	7	64.00	3-91	-
LS Birkett	21	1	71	1	71.00	1-16	-
GC Grant	1	-	1	0	-	-	-
JED Sealy	3	-	32	0	-	-	-

West Indians' averages in all first-class matches

Batsman	M	Inns	NO	HS	Runs	Av	100	50	C/S
GA Headley	13	25	1	131	1066	44.41	4	4	7
JED Sealy	8	13	4	92	334	37.11	-	2	11
GC Grant	14	24	4	102	739	36.95	1	5	11
LN Constantine	13	23	-	100	708	30.78	1	5	21
FR Martin	13	24	2	123*	606	27.54	1	2	2
LS Birkett	11	20	1	128*	499	26.26	1	1	10
CA Roach	14	26	-	104	637	24.50	1	3	10
FI de Caires	4	7	-	76	165	23.57	-	2	2
EAC Hunte	5	9	2	29	135	19.28	-	-	6/2
OC Scott	12	19	5	67*	251	17.92	-	1	-
IM Barrow	9	15	1	45	245	17.50	-	-	15/3
EL Bartlett	8	13	1	84	208	17.33	-	1	2
OS Wight	3	6	-	22	45	7.50	-	-	-
GN Francis	11	17	4	16*	92	7.07	-	-	7
HC Griffith	12	17	4	17	92	7.07	-	-	4
EL St Hill	4	6	1	9	16	3.20	-	-	2

Bowler	Balls	M	Runs	W	Av	Best	5w
FI de Caires	32	-	20	1	20.00	1-20	-
LN Constantine	1802	25	950	47	20.21	6-25	3
GN Francis	1748	38	840	29	28.96	4-48	-
EL St Hill	907	10	477	16	29.81	4-57	-
OC Scott	2130	10	1325	40	33.12	5-63	2
HC Griffith	2210	42	1107	31	35.70	4-50	-
FR Martin	2338	46	950	21	45.23	3-35	-
JED Sealy	194	2	127	2	63.50	1-4	-
LS Birkett	366	2	205	2	102.50	1-16	-
GC Grant	6	-	1	0	-	-	-
GA Headley	56	-	39	0	-	-	-
CA Roach	88	1	63	0	-	-	-

The Sheffield Shield in 1930-31

Scores

31 October, 1, 3 November 1930, at Brisbane. Queensland 289 (M Biggs 108, FC Thompson 78, TA Carlton 4-67, PK Lee 4-98) and 88 for 3 (M Biggs 47) beat South Australia 72 (HM Thurlow 5-25) and 304 (PK Lee 57 not out, HC Nitschke 54, DE Pritchard 52, RK Oxenham 3-60). Queensland 5 points, South Australia 0.

7, 8, 10, 11 November 1930, at Sydney. New South Wales 228 (AG Fairfax 62, DG Bradman 61, JEH Hooker 54, TA Carlton 4-28, CS Deverson 4-60) and 396 (DG Bradman 121, AF Kippax 104, AH Allsopp 93, CS Deverson 4-86) beat South Australia 124 (PK Lee 40, JEH Hooker 5-28, GL Stewart 3-25) and 287 (HC Nitschke 141, AG Fairfax 4-54, WA Hunt 3-37). New South Wales 5 points, South Australia 0.

28, 29 November, 1, 2 December 1930, at Brisbane. New South Wales 566 (SJ McCabe 161 AF Kippax 158 OW Bill 153, E Gilbert 4-118, A Hurwood 3-108) and 159 for 5 (A Jackson 53, SJ McCabe 53, RK Okenham 4-19) drew with Queensland 687 (FC Thompson 275 not out, FJ Gough 137, RK Oxenham 67, EC Bensted 52, A Hurwood 47, WA Hunt 4-128). Queensland 3 points, New South Wales 1.

11, 12, 14, 15 December 1930, at Sydney. Queensland 166 (VHV Goodwin 62, RK Oxenham 53, WA Hunt 5-37) and 369 (EC Bensted 92, VHV Goodwin 64, FJ Gough 58, JEH Hooker 4-63) drew with New South Wales 143 (JHW Fingleton 56, E Gilbert 4-44) and 212 for one (OW Bill 93 not out, JHW Fingleton 71). Queensland 3 points, New South Wales 1.

18, 19, 20, 22 December 1930, at Adelaide. New South Wales 610 (DG Bradman 258, A Jackson 166, JEH Hooker 45, AF Kippax 42, CV Grimmett 5-180) beat South Australia 166 (HC Nitschke 69, WA Hunt 5-36, HC Chilvers 5-68) and 310 (HC Nitschke 102, TW Wall 45 not out, WA Hunt 4-105, DG Bradman 3-54). New South Wales 5 points South Australia 0.

18, 19, 20 December, at Melbourne. Victoria 474 (KE Rigg 124, J Ryder 114, EL a'Beckett 92, LPJ O'Brien 65, RK Oxenham 6-92) beat Queensland 103 (H Ironmonger 5-29, DDJ Blackie 3-37) and 129 (EC Bensted 40, H Ironmonger 6-41, DDJ Blackie 4-57). Victoria 5 points, Queensland 0.

24, 26, 27, 29 December 1930, at Melbourne. Victoria 185 (WH Ponsford 109, AG Fairfax 4-41) drew with New South Wales 97 for 6 (A Jackson 52 not out). Victoria 2 points, New South Wales 2 points.

25, 26 December 1930, at Adelaide. South Australia 305 (HC Nitschke 142, BJ Tobin 40, RK Oxenham 6-51) beat Queensland 124 (FC Thompson 50, CV Grimmett 4-23) and 117 (CV Grimmett 5-31).

1, 2, 3, 5 January 1931, at Melbourne. South Australia 275 (VY Richardson 64, MG Waite 44, HC Nitschke 43, DDJ Blackie 6-70) and 353 for 8 declared (AR Lonergan 100 not out, AT Hack 87, MG Waite 59) drew with Victoria 386 (HH Oakley 108, LPJ O'Brien 75, BA Barnett 54, J Ryder 49, PK Lee 5-106, TA Carlton 4-91) and 85 for 7 (TA Carlton 3-28). Victoria 3 points South Australia 1.

24, 26, 27, 28 January 1931, at Sydney. New South Wales 196 (AG Fairfax 46, DDJ Blackie 4-45, HH Alexander 3-43) and 417 for 9 declared (DG Bradman 220, OW Bill 100, DDJ Blackie 5-101, H Ironmonger 3-91) drew with Victoria 318 (LPJ O'Brien 119, SJ McCabe 4-46) and 202 for 6 (KE Rigg 98, WA Hunt 3-38). Victoria 3 points, New South Wales 1.

31 January, 2, 3, 4 February 1931, at Brisbane. The match between Queensland and Victoria was abandoned without a ball bowled. Queensland 2 points, Victoria 2 points.

20, 21, 23, 24 February 1931, at Adelaide. South Australia 439 (AR Lonergan 159, MG Waite 74, CW Walker 44 not out, H Ironmonger 7-135) and 154 (H Ironmonger 5-60) drew with Victoria 369 (WM Woodfull 177, HH Oakley 73, KE Rigg 50, CV Grimmett 4-105, PK Lee 3-67) and 131 for 4 (J Ryder 48 not out, BJ Tobin 3-26). South Australia 3 points, Victoria 1.

Final points: Victoria 16, New South Wales 15, Queensland 13, South Australia 9.

Leading first-class averages in Australia, 1930-31

Batsman	M	Inns	NO	HS	Runs	Av	100	50
FC Thompson (Q)	5	8	2	275*	475	79.16	1	2
DG Bradman (NSW/A)	12	18	-	258	1422	79.00	5	4
WH Ponsford (V/A)	9	13	2	187	816	74.18	4	1
J Ryder (V)	7	11	3	114	458	57.25	1	2
HC Nitschke (SA)	9	16	1	142	830	55.33	4	2
KE Rigg (V/A)	7	11	-	126	561	51.00	2	3
AF Kippax (NSW/A)	13	18	-	158	902	50.11	4	2
AR Lonergan (SA)	7	12	1	159	541	49.18	2	2
DC Green (Tas)	6	9	-	147	442	49.11	1	1
WM Woodfull (V/A)	9	12	2	177	477	47.70	1	3
A Jackson (NSW/A)	9	13	2	166	502	45.63	1	4
GA Headley (WI)	13	25	1	131	1066	44.41	4	4
VHV Goodwin (Q)	4	8	1	64	297	42.42	-	4
OW Bill (NSW)	7	13	1	153	503	41.91	2	1
SJ McCabe (NSW/A)	12	18	1	161	704	41.41	2	2
JED Sealy (WI)	8	13	4	92	334	37.11	-	2
GC Grant (WI)	14	24	4	102	739	36.95	1	5
PK Lee (SA)	9	15	2	106	479	36.84	1	3
LJ Nash (Tas)	6	9	-	110	329	36.55	1	2
AG Fairfax (NSW/A)	12	17	4	62	463	35.61	-	3

Bowler	Balls	M	Runs	W	Av	Best	5w
H Ironmonger (V/A)	2713	112	972	68	14.29	8-31	7
DDJ Blackie (V)	1280	24	470	29	16.20	6-70	2
RK Oxenham (Q/A)	2166	110	602	33	18.24	6-51	2
CV Grimmett (SA/A)	3524	100	1417	74	19.14	7-87	7
LN Constantine (WI)	1802	25	950	47	20.21	6-25	3
TA Carlton (SA)	1900	60	663	31	21.38	4-22	-
JEH Hooker (NSW)	1246	31	323	15	21.53	5-28	1
AC Newton (Tas)	584	8	218	10	21.80	4-36	-
WA Hunt (NSW)	1996	46	712	32	22.25	5-36	2
LJ Nash (Tas)	1003	8	492	20	24.60	5-65	2
CS Deverson (Tas)	480	2	255	10	25.50	4-60	-
A Hurwood (Q/A)	1053	34	428	16	26.75	4-22	-
PK Lee (SA)	1968	35	859	32	26.84	5-57	2
E Gilbert (Q)	1342	18	593	22	26.95	5-65	1
GN Francis (WI)	1748	38	840	29	28.96	4-48	-

A note on sources

In 1954, George Headley began work on a draft autobiography. The book was never completed. It appears to have been prepared in meetings with CLR James, who took down Headley's account of events and turned them into a manuscript. When James completed each part of the manuscript, he sent it to Headley and Learie Constantine to be checked. The draft is part of the CLR James papers in the Alma Jordan Library at the University of the West indies. Some of the statements I have attributed to George Headley are taken from this draft autobiography.

The quotes from Lionel Birkett and Doug Green are taken from The West Indies in Australia, 1930-31 by Brian Bassano and Rick Smith.

Most of the statements attributed to Jack Grant are extracted from his posthumous autobiography, Jack Grant's Book, although others come from contemporary newspaper reports.

Otherwise, where quotes are attributed to players, they are usually taken from contemporary newspaper reports.

It's possible that enlightening information about the tour is contained in the archival minutes and correspondence of Cricket Australia. Unfortunately, as at the date of publication, Cricket Australia had mislaid, and was unable to locate, that material.

Select bibliography

Brian Bassano and Rick Smith, The West Indies in Australia, 1930-31, Tasmania, 1990

Joan Beaumont, Australia's Great Depression, Sydney, 2022

Hilary McD Beckles and Brian Stoddart, Liberation Cricket: West Indies cricket culture, Manchester, 1995

Mike Colman, Eddie Gilbert, the true story of an aboriginal cricketing legend, Sydney, 2002

Learie Constantine, Cricket in the Sun, London, 1948

Learie Constantine, Colour Bar, London, 1954

David Frith, Archie Jackson, the Keats of Cricket, London, 1987

David Frith, Frith's Encounters, London, 2014

GC Grant, Jack Grant's Book, London, 1980

Gideon Haigh and David Frith, Inside Story, Melbourne, 2007
Gerald Howat, Learie Constantine, London, 1975
CLR James, Beyond A Boundary, London, 1963
Bede Nairn, The Big Fella: Jack Lang and the Australian Labor Party, 1891-1949, Melbourne, 1986
Michael Manley, A History of West Indies Cricket, London, 1988
Wisden's Cricketers' Almanack, various years

Newspapers

The Advertiser; The Age; The Argus; The Australasian; The Barbados Advocate; The Brisbane Courier; The Daily Chronicle; The Daily News; The Daily Pictorial; The Daily Standard; The Evening News; The Evening Post; The Evening Star; The Examiner; The Herald; The Jamaica Guardian; The Jamaica Times; The Kingston Gleaner; The Labor Daily; The Mail; The Mercury; The Mirror; The Observer; The Newcastle Sun; News; The Port of Spain Gazette; The Press; The Queensland Times; The Recorder; The Referee; The Register News Pictorial; The Sporting Globe; The Sun; The Sunday Pictorial; The Sydney Mail; The Sydney Morning Herald; The Telegraph; The Trinidad Sporting Chronicle; Truth; The Workman.

Magazines

The Australian Cricketer; The Bulletin; The Cricketer.

Acknowledgments

The author acknowledges with thanks the assistance of the staff of the Mitchell Library, British Library, National Archives of Australia and Alma Jordan Library at the University of the West Indies.

Isabelle de Caires provided invaluable information concerning the de Caires family.

INDEX

Printed in Australia
Ingram Content Group Australia Pty Ltd
AUHW020911310724
397773AU00002B/3

9 781923 024953